The Dh

The Buddha's

Translated from the Pāli by
Acharya Buddharakkhita

Introduction by
Bhikkhu Bodhi

BPE

BPS Pariyatti Editions

BPS Pariyatti Editions
An imprint of Pariyatti Publishing
www.pariyatti.org

First BPS Pariyatti Edition, 2019
ISBN: 978-1-68172-273-3 (Print)
ISBN: 978-1-68172-276-4 (PDF)
ISBN: 978-1-68172-274-0 (ePub)
ISBN: 978-1-68172-275-7 (Mobi)
LCCN: 2019947278

Contents

Preface

The Dhammapada is the best known and most widely esteemed text in the Pāli Tipiṭaka, the sacred scriptures of Theravāda Buddhism. The work is included in the Khuddaka Nikāya ("Minor Collection") of the Sutta Piṭaka, but its popularity has raised it far above the single niche it occupies in the scriptures to the ranks of a world religious classic. Composed in the ancient Pāli language, this slim anthology of verses constitutes a perfect compendium of the Buddha's teaching, comprising between its covers all the essential principles elaborated at length in the forty-odd volumes of the Pāli Canon.

According to the Theravāda Buddhist tradition, each verse in the Dhammapada was originally spoken by the Buddha in response to a particular episode. Accounts of these, along with exegeses of the verses, are preserved in the classic commentary to the work, compiled by the great scholiast Bhadantācariya Buddhaghosa in the fifth century C.E. on the basis of material going back to very ancient times. The contents of the verses, however, transcend the limited and particular circumstances of their origin, reaching out through the ages to various types of people in all the diverse situations of life. For the simple and unsophisticated the Dhammapada is a sympathetic counsellor; for the intellectually overburdened, its clear and direct teachings inspire humility and reflection; for the earnest seeker, it is a perennial source of inspiration and practical instruction. Insights that flashed into the heart of the Buddha have crystallized into these luminous verses of pure wisdom. As profound expressions of practical spirituality, each verse is a guideline to right living. The Buddha unambiguously pointed out that whoever earnestly practises the teachings found in the Dhammapada will taste the bliss of emancipation.

Due to its immense importance, the Dhammapada has been translated into numerous languages. In English alone many translations are available, including editions by such noted scholars as Max Müller and Dr. S. Radhakrishnan. However, when translated by non-Buddhists, the Dhammapada has suffered from some distortion: an unfortunate selection of renderings has sometimes suggested erroneous interpretations, while footnotes have tended to be judgemental.

The present translation was originally made in the late 1950's. Some years earlier, while consulting a number of English translations of the Dhammapada, I noticed that the renderings were either inaccurate or too pedantic, and I therefore felt that a new translation avoiding these two extremes would serve a valuable purpose. The finished result of that project, presented here, is a humble attempt by a practising follower of the Buddha to transmit the spirit and content, as well as the language and style, of the original teachings.

In preparing this volume I have had access to numerous editions of the Pāli text and to translations of the Dhammapada into various languages, including Sanskrit, Hindi, Bengali, Sinhala, Burmese, and Nepali. I particularly benefitted from the excellent translations by the late Venerable Nārada Mahāthera of Vajirārāma, Colombo, and Professor Bhagwat of Poona; to them I acknowledge my debt. The Pāli text has been prepared on the basis of several existing editions in different scripts, but it relies most upon the Burmese-script Sixth Buddhist Council edition published in Rangoon. A few verses contain riddles, references, or analogies that may not be evident to the reader. The meanings of these are provided either in parenthesis or in the notes, and for their interpretation I have relied on the explanations given in Bhadantācariya Buddhaghosa's commentary.

A first edition of this translation was published in 1959 and a second in 1966, both by the Maha Bodhi Society in Bangalore, India. A third edition, substantially revised, was published by the Buddhist Publication Society in 1985. For the present fourth edition, the translation has again undergone considerable revision. The subtitle, "The Buddha's Path of Wisdom," is not literal, but serves to show that the verses of the Dhammapada all originate from the Buddha's wisdom and lead the one who follows them to a life guided by that same wisdom.

I am grateful to the editors of the Buddhist Publication Society for their helpful suggestions, and to the Society itself for so generously undertaking the publication of this work.

I make this offering of Dhamma in grateful memory of my teachers, parents, and relatives, departed and living. May they find access in the Buddha's Dispensation and attain Nibbāna!

May all beings be happy!
Acharya Buddharakkhita

The Pali Alphabet

Vowels:	a, ā, i, ī, u, ū, e, o
Consonants:	
Gutterals:	k, kh, g, gh, ṅ
Palatals:	c, ch, j, jh, ñ
Cerebrals:	ṭ, ṭh, ḍ, ḍh, ṇ
Dentals:	t, th, d, dh, n
Labials:	p, ph, b, bh, m
Other:	y, r, l, ḷ, v, s, h, ṃ

Pronunciation:

a as in "cut"
ā as in "father"
i as in "king"
ī as in "keen"

Of the vowels, e and o are long before a single consonant and short before a double consonant. Among the consonants, g is pronounced as in "good," c as in "church," ñ as in "canyon." The cerebrals (also called retroflexes)— ṭ, ṭh, ḍ, ḍh, ṇ, ḷ— are spoken with the tongue on the roof of the mouth; the dentals—t, th, d, dh, n, l—with the tongue on the upper teeth. The aspirates—kh, gh, ch, jh, ṭh, ḍh, th, dh, ph, bh—are single consonants pronounced with a slight outward puff of breath, e.g. th as in "Thomas" (not as in "thin"), ph as in "putter" (not as in "phone"). Double consonants are always enunciated separately, e.g. dd as in "mad dog," gg as in "big gun." The pure nasal (niggahīta) ṃ is pronounced like the ng in "song." An o and an e always carry a stress; otherwise the stress falls on a long vowel—ā, ī, ū—or on a double consonant, or on ṃ.

Introduction

From ancient times to the present, the Dhammapada has been regarded as the most succinct expression of the Buddha's Teaching found in the Pāli Canon and the chief spiritual testament of early Buddhism. In the countries following Theravāda Buddhism, such as Sri Lanka, Burma, and Thailand, the influence of the Dhammapada is ubiquitous. It is an ever-fecund source of themes for sermons and discussions, a guidebook for resolving the countless problems of everyday life, a primer for the instruction of novices in the monasteries. Even the experienced contemplative, withdrawn to forest hermitage or mountainside cave for a life of meditation, can be expected to count a copy of the book among his few material possessions. Yet the admiration the Dhammapada has elicited has not been confined to avowed followers of Buddhism. Wherever it has become known its moral earnestness, realistic understanding of human life, aphoristic wisdom, and stirring message of a way to freedom from suffering have won for it the devotion and veneration of those responsive to the good and the true.

The expounder of the verses that comprise the Dhammapada is the Indian sage called the Buddha, an honorific title meaning "the Enlightened One" or "the Awakened One." The story of this venerable personage has often been overlaid with literary embellishment and the admixture of legend, but the historical essentials of his life are simple and clear. He was born in the sixth century B.C., the son of a king ruling over a small state in the Himalayan foothills, in what is now Nepal. His given name was Siddhattha and his family name Gotama (Sanskrit: Siddhārtha Gautama). Raised in luxury, groomed by his father to be the heir to the throne, in his early manhood he went through a deeply disturbing encounter with the sufferings of life, as a result of which he lost all interest in the pleasures and privileges of rulership. One night, in his twenty-ninth year, he fled the royal city and entered the forest to live as an ascetic, resolved to find a way to deliverance from suffering. For six years he experimented with different systems of meditation and subjected himself to severe austerities, but found that these practices did not bring him any closer to his goal. Finally, in his thirty-fifth year, while sitting in deep meditation beneath a tree at Gayā, he attained Supreme Enlightenment and became, in the proper sense of the title, the Buddha, the Enlightened One. Thereafter, for forty-five years, he travelled throughout northern India, proclaiming the truths he had discovered and founding an order of monks and nuns to carry on his message. At the age of eighty, after a long and fruitful life, he passed away peacefully in the small town of Kusinārā, surrounded by a large number of disciples.

To his followers, the Buddha is neither a god, nor a divine incarnation, nor a prophet bearing a message of divine revelation, but a human being who by his own striving and intelligence has reached the highest spiritual attainment of which man is capable—perfect wisdom, full enlightenment, complete purification of mind. His function in relation to humanity is that of a teacher—a world teacher who, out of compassion, points out to others the way to Nibbāna (Sanskrit: Nirvāṇa), final release from suffering. His teaching, known as the Dhamma, offers a body of instructions explaining the true nature of existence and showing the path that leads to liberation. Free from all dogmas and inscrutable claims to authority, the Dhamma is founded solidly upon the bedrock of the Buddha's own clear comprehension of reality, and it leads the one who practises it to that same understanding—the knowledge that extricates the roots of suffering.

The title "Dhammapada" which the ancient compilers of the Buddhist scriptures attached to our anthology means portions, aspects, or sections of Dhamma. The work has been given this title because, in its twenty-six chapters, it spans the multiple aspects of the Buddha's teaching, offering a variety of standpoints from which to gain a glimpse into its heart. Whereas the longer discourses of the Buddha contained in the prose sections of the Canon usually proceed methodically, unfolding according to the sequential structure of the doctrine, the Dhammapada lacks any such systematic arrangement. The work is simply a collection of inspirational or pedagogical verses on the fundamentals of the Teaching, to be used as a basis for personal edification and instruction. In any given chapter several successive verses may have been spoken by the Buddha on a single occasion, and thus among themselves will exhibit a meaningful development or a set of variations on a theme. But by and large, the logic behind the grouping together of verses into a chapter is merely the concern with a common topic. The twenty-six chapter headings thus function as a kind of rubric for classifying the diverse poetic utterances of the Master, and the reason behind the inclusion of any given verse in a particular chapter is its mention of the subject indicated in the chapter's heading. In some cases (Chapters 4 and 23) this may be a metaphorical symbol rather than a point of doctrine. There also seems to be no intentional design in the order of the chapters themselves, though at certain points a loose thread of development can be discerned.

The teachings of the Buddha, viewed in their completeness, all fit together into a single perfectly coherent system of thought and practice which gains its unity from its final goal, the attainment of deliverance from suffering. But the teachings inevitably emerge from the human condition as their matrix and starting point, and therefore must be expressed in such a way as to reach human beings standing at different levels of spiritual development, with their highly diverse problems, ends, and concerns, and with their very different capacities for understanding. Thus, just as water, though one in essence, assumes different shapes due to the vessels into which it is poured, so the Dhamma of liberation takes on different forms in response to the needs of the beings to be taught. This diversity, evident enough already in the prose discourses, becomes even more conspicuous in the highly condensed, spontaneous, and intuitively charged medium of verse used in the Dhammapada. The intensified power of delivery can result in apparent inconsistencies which may perplex the unwary.

For example, in many verses the Buddha commends certain practices on the grounds that they lead to a heavenly birth, but in others he discourages disciples from aspiring for heaven and extols the one who takes no delight in celestial pleasures (187, 417).[1] Often he enjoins works of merit, yet elsewhere he praises the one who has gone beyond both merit and demerit (39, 412). Without a grasp of the underlying structure of the Dhamma, such statements viewed side by side will appear incompatible and may even elicit the judgement that the teaching is self-contradictory.

The key to resolving these apparent discrepancies is the recognition that the Dhamma assumes its formulation from the needs of the diverse persons to whom it is addressed, as well as from the diversity of needs that may co-exist even in a single individual. To make sense of the various utterances found in the Dhammapada, I will sketch a schematism of four levels to be used for ascertaining the intention behind any particular verse found in the work, and thus for understanding its proper place in the total systematic vision of the Dhamma. This fourfold schematism develops out of an

ancient interpretive maxim which holds that the Buddha's Teaching is designed to meet three primary aims: human welfare here and now, a favourable rebirth in the next life, and the attainment of the ultimate good. The four levels are arrived at by distinguishing the last aim into two stages: path and fruit.

1. The Human Good Here and Now

The first level of instruction found in the Dhammapada is addressed to the need to establish human well-being and happiness in the immediately visible sphere of concrete human relations. The aim at this level is to show us the way to live at peace with ourselves and our fellows, to fulfil our family and social responsibilities, and to restrain the bitterness, conflict, and violence which infest human relationships and bring such

1. Unless chapter numbers are given, figures in parenthesis refer to verse numbers of the Dhammapada.

immense suffering to the individual, society, and the world as a whole. The guidelines appropriate to this level are largely identical with the basic ethical injunctions proposed by most of the great world religions, but in the Buddhist teaching they are freed from theistic moorings and grounded upon two directly verifiable foundations: (i) concern for one's own integrity and long-range happiness, and (ii) concern for the welfare of those whom one's actions may affect (129–132).

The most general counsel the Dhammapada gives is to avoid all evil, to cultivate good, and to cleanse one's mind (183). But to dispel any doubts the disciple might entertain as to what one should avoid and what one should cultivate, other verses provide more specific directives. One should avoid irritability in deed, word, and thought and exercise self-control (231–234). One should adhere to the Five Precepts, the fundamental moral code of Buddhism, which teach abstinence from destroying life, from stealing, from committing adultery, from speaking lies, and from taking intoxicants; one who violates these five training rules "digs up his own root even in this very world" (246–247). The disciple should treat all beings with kindness and compassion, live honestly and righteously, control sensual desire, speak the truth, and live a sober upright life, diligently fulfilling his duties, such as service to parents, to his immediate family, and to those recluses and brahmins who depend on the laity for their maintenance (332–333).

A large number of verses pertaining to this first level are concerned with the resolution of conflict and hostility. Quarrels are to be avoided by patience and forgiveness, for responding to hatred by further hatred only maintains the cycle of vengeance and retaliation. The true conquest of hatred is achieved by non-hatred, by forbearance, by love (4–6). One should not respond to bitter speech but maintain silence (134). One should not yield to anger but control it as a driver controls a chariot (222). Instead of keeping watch for the faults of others, the disciple is admonished to examine his own faults and to make a continual effort to remove his impurities just as a silversmith purifies silver (50, 239). Even if one has committed evil in the past, there is no need for dejection or despair; for our destinies can be radically changed, and one who abandons the evil for the good illuminates this world like the moon freed from a cloud (173).

The sterling qualities distinguishing the superior person (*sappurisa*) are generosity, truthfulness, patience, and compassion (223). By developing and mastering these qualities within ourselves, we can live in harmony with our own conscience and at peace with our fellow beings. The scent of virtue, the Buddha declares, is sweeter than the scent of all flowers and perfumes; the good man or woman shines from afar like the Himalayan mountains; just as the lotus flower rises up in all its beauty above the muck and mire of the roadside refuse heap, so does the disciple of the Buddha rise up in splendour of wisdom above the masses of ignorant worldlings (54, 304, 59).

2. The Good in Future Lives

In its second level of teaching, the Dhammapada shows that morality does not exhaust its significance in its contribution to human felicity here and now, but exercises a far more critical influence in moulding personal destiny. This level begins with the recognition that, to reflective thought, the human situation demands a more satisfactory context for ethics than mere appeals to altruism can provide. On the one hand, our innate sense of moral justice requires that goodness be recompensed with happiness and evil with suffering; on the other, our typical experience shows us virtuous people beset with hardships and afflictions and thoroughly bad people riding the waves of fortune (119–120). Moral intuition tells us that if there is any long-range value to righteousness, the imbalance must somehow be redressed. The visible order does not yield an evident solution, but the Buddha's Teaching reveals the factor needed to vindicate our cry for moral justice in an impersonal universal law which reigns over all sentient existence. This is the law of kamma (Sanskrit: *karma*), of action and its fruit, which ensures that morally determinate action does not disappear into nothingness but eventually meets its due retribution, the good with happiness, the bad with suffering.

In the popular understanding kamma is sometimes identified with fate, but this is a total misconception utterly inapplicable to the Buddhist doctrine. Kamma means volitional action, action springing from intention, which may manifest itself outwardly as bodily deeds or speech, or remain internally as unexpressed thoughts, desires, and emotions. The Buddha distinguishes kamma into two primary ethical types: unwholesome kamma, action rooted in mental states of greed, hatred, and delusion; and wholesome kamma, action rooted in mental states of generosity or detachment, goodwill, and understanding. The willed actions we perform in the course of our lives may fade from memory without a trace, but once performed they leave subtle imprints on the mind, seeds with the potential to come to fruition in the future when they meet conditions conducive to their ripening.

The objective field in which the seeds of kamma ripen is the process of rebirths called saṃsāra. In the Buddha's Teaching, life is not viewed as an isolated occurrence beginning spontaneously with birth and ending in utter annihilation at death. Each single lifespan is seen, rather, as part of an individualized series of lives having no discoverable beginning in time and continuing on as long as the desire for existence stands intact. Rebirth can take place in various realms. There are not only the familiar realms of human beings and animals, but ranged above we meet heavenly worlds of greater happiness, beauty, and power, and ranged below infernal worlds of extreme suffering.

The cause for rebirth into these various realms the Buddha locates in kamma, our own willed actions. In its primary role, kamma determines the sphere into which rebirth takes place, wholesome actions bringing rebirth in higher forms, unwholesome actions rebirth in lower forms. After yielding rebirth, kamma continues to operate, governing the endowments and circumstances of the individual within the given form of existence. Thus, within the human world, previous stores of wholesome kamma will issue in long life, health, wealth, beauty, and success; stores of unwholesome kamma in short life, illness, poverty, ugliness, and failure.

Prescriptively, the second level of teaching found in the Dhammapada is the practical corollary to this recognition of the law of kamma, put forth to show human beings, who naturally desire happiness and freedom from sorrow, the effective means to achieve their objectives. The content of this teaching itself does not differ from that presented at the first level; it is the same set of ethical injunctions for abstaining from evil and for cultivating the good. The difference lies in the perspective from which the injunctions are issued and the aim for the sake of which they are to be taken up. The principles of morality are shown now in their broader cosmic connections, as tied to an invisible but all-embracing law which binds together all life and holds sway over the repeated rotations of the cycle of birth and death. The observance of morality is justified, despite its difficulties and apparent failures, by the fact that it is in harmony with that law, that through the efficacy of kamma our willed actions become the chief determinant of our destiny both in this life and in future states of becoming. To follow the ethical law leads upwards—to inner purification, to higher rebirths, and to richer experiences of happiness and joy. To violate the law, to act in the grip of selfishness and hate, leads downwards—to inner deterioration, to suffering, and to rebirth in the worlds of misery. This theme is announced already by the pair of verses which opens the Dhammapada, and reappears in diverse formulations throughout the work (see e.g. 15–18, 117–122, 127, 132–133, Chapter 22).

3. The Path to the Final Goal

The teaching on kamma and rebirth, with its practical corollary that we should perform deeds of merit with the aim of obtaining a higher mode of rebirth, is not by any means the final message of the Buddha or the decisive counsel of the Dhammapada. In its own sphere of application, this teaching is perfectly valid as a preparatory or provisional measure for those whose spiritual faculties are not yet ripe but still require further maturation over a succession of lives. A deeper, more searching examination, however, reveals that all states of existence in saṃsāra, even the loftiest celestial abodes, are lacking in genuine worth; for they are all inherently impermanent, without any lasting substance, and thus, for those who cling to them, potential bases for suffering. The disciple of mature faculties, sufficiently prepared by previous experience for the Buddha's distinctive exposition of the Dhamma, does not long even for rebirth among the gods. Having understood the intrinsic inadequacy of all conditioned things, his sole aspiration is for deliverance from the ever-repeating round of births. This is the ultimate goal to which the Buddha points, as the immediate aim for those of developed faculties and also as the long-term ideal for those in need of further development: Nibbāna, the Deathless, the unconditioned state where there is no more birth, ageing, and death, and thus no more suffering.

The third level of teaching found in the Dhammapada sets forth the theoretical framework and practical discipline emerging out of the aspiration for final deliverance. The theoretical framework is provided by the teaching of the Four Noble Truths (190–192, 273), which the Buddha had proclaimed already in his first sermon and upon which he placed so much stress in his many discourses that all schools of Buddhism have appropriated them as their common foundation. The four truths all centre around the fact of suffering (*dukkha*), understood not as mere experienced pain and sorrow, but as the pervasive unsatisfactoriness of everything conditioned (202–203). The first truth details the various forms of suffering—birth, old age, sickness and death, the misery of unpleasant encounters and painful separations, the suffering of not obtaining what one wants. It culminates in the declaration that all constituent phenomena of body and mind, "the five aggregates of existence" (*pañcakkhandhā*), being impermanent and substanceless, are intrinsically unsatisfactory. The second truth points out that the cause of suffering is craving (*taṇhā*), the desire for pleasure and existence which drives us through the round of rebirths, bringing in its trail sorrow, anxiety, and despair (212–216, Chapter 24). The third truth declares that the destruction of craving issues in release from suffering, and the fourth prescribes the means to release, the Noble Eightfold Path: right understanding, right thought, right speech, right action, right livelihood, right effort, right mindfulness, and right concentration (Chapter 20).

If, at this third level, the doctrinal emphasis shifts from the principles of kamma and rebirth to the Four Noble Truths, a corresponding shift in emphasis takes place in the practical sphere as well. The stress now no longer falls on the observation of basic morality and the cultivation of wholesome attitudes as a means to higher rebirths. Instead it falls on the integral development of the Noble Eightfold Path as the means to uproot the craving that nurtures the process of rebirth itself. For practical purposes the eight factors of the path are arranged into three major groups which reveal more clearly the developmental structure of the training: moral discipline (including right speech, right action, and right livelihood); concentration (including right effort, right mindfulness, and right concentration); and wisdom (including right understanding and right thought). By the training in morality, the coarsest forms of the mental defilements, those erupting as unwholesome deeds and words, are checked and kept under control. By the training in concentration the mind is made calm, pure, and unified, purged of the currents of distractive thoughts. By the training in wisdom the concentrated beam of attention is focused upon the constituent factors of mind and body to investigate and contemplate their salient characteristics. This wisdom, gradually ripened, culminates in the understanding that brings complete purification and deliverance of mind.

In principle, the practice of the path in all three stages is feasible for people in any walk of life. The Buddha taught it to lay people as well as to monks, and many of his lay followers reached high stages of attainment. However, application to the development of the path becomes most fruitful for those who have relinquished all other concerns in order to devote themselves wholeheartedly to spiritual training, to living the "holy life" (*brahmacariya*). For conduct to be completely purified, for sustained contemplation and penetrating wisdom to unfold without impediments, the adoption of a different lifestyle becomes imperative, one which minimizes distractions and stimulants to craving and orders all activities around the aim of liberation. Thus the Buddha established the Sangha, the order of monks and nuns, as the special field for those ready to dedicate their lives to the practice of the path.

In the Dhammapada we find the call to the monastic life resounding throughout. The entry way to the monastic life is an act of radical renunciation spurred on by our confrontation with suffering, particularly by our recognition of our inevitable mortality. The Dhammapada teaches that just as a cowherd drives the cattle to pasture, so old age and death drive living beings from life to life (135). There is no place in the world where one can escape death, for death is stamped into the very substance of our being (128). The body is a painted mirage in which there is nothing lasting or stable; it is a mass of sores, a nest of disease, which breaks up and ends in death; it is a city built of bones containing within itself decay and death; the foolish are attached to it, but the wise, having seen that the body ends as a corpse, lose all delight in mundane joys (146–150).

Having recognized the transience and hidden misery of mundane life, the thoughtful break the ties of family and social relationships, abandon their homes and sensual pleasures, and enter upon the state of -homelessness: "Like swans that abandon the lake, they leave home after home behind.... Having gone from home to homelessness, they delight in detachment so difficult to enjoy" (91, 87). Withdrawn to silent and secluded places, the renunciants seek out the company of wise instructors, who point out their faults, who admonish and instruct them and shield them from wrong, who show them the right path (76–78, 208). Under their guidance, they live by the rules of the monastic order, content with the simplest material requisites, moderate in eating, practising patience and forbearance, devoted to meditation (184–185). Having learned to still the restless waves of thought and to gain one-pointed concentration, they go on to contemplate the arising and falling away of all formations: "The monk who has retired to a solitary abode and calmed the mind, comprehends the Dhamma with insight, and there arises in him a delight that transcends all human delights. Whenever he sees with insight the rise and fall of the aggregates, he is full of joy and happiness" (373, 374).

The life of meditation reaches its peak in the development of insight, and the Dhammapada succinctly enunciates the principles to be seen with the wisdom of insight: "All conditioned things are impermanent ... All conditioned things are suffering ... All things are not self. When one sees this with wisdom, then one turns away from suffering. This is the path to purification" (277–279). When these truths are penetrated by direct vision, the fetters of attachment break asunder, and the disciple rises through successive stages of realization to the attainment of full liberation.

4. The Highest Goal

The fourth level of teaching in the Dhammapada does not reveal any new principles of doctrine or approaches to practice. This level shows us, rather, the fruit of the third level. The third level discloses the path to the highest goal, the way to break free from all bondage and suffering and to win the supreme peace of Nibbāna. The fourth level is a celebration and acclamation of those who have gained the fruits of the path and won the final goal.

In the Pāli Canon the stages of definite attainment along the way to Nibbāna are enumerated as four. At the first, called "stream-entry" (*sotāpatti*), the disciple gains a first glimpse of "the Deathless" and enters irreversibly upon the path to liberation, bound to reach the goal in seven lives at most. This achievement alone, the Dhammapada declares, is greater than lordship over all the worlds (178). Following stream-entry come two further stages which weaken and eradicate still more defilements and bring the goal increasingly closer to view. One is called the stage of once-returner (*sakadāgāmī*), when the disciple will return to the human world at most only one more time; the other the stage of non-returner (*anāgāmī*), when he will never come back to human existence but will take rebirth in a celestial plane, bound to win final deliverance there. The fourth and final stage is that of the arahat, the Perfected One, the fully accomplished sage who has completed the development of the path, eradicated all defilements, and broken free from bondage to the cycle of rebirths. This is the ideal figure of early Buddhism and the supreme hero of the Dhammapada.

The arahat is depicted in two full chapters: in Chapter 7 under his own name and in Chapter 26, the last chapter, under the name "brāhmaṇa," the holy man. We are told that the arahat is no longer troubled by the fever of the passions; he is sorrowless and wholly set free; he has broken all ties. His taints are destroyed: he is not attached to food; his field is the void and unconditioned freedom. For ordinary worldlings the arahat is incomprehensible: his path cannot be traced, like that of birds in the sky. He has transcended all worldliness, passed beyond sorrow and lamentation, become peaceful and fearless. He is free from anger, devout, virtuous, without craving, self-subdued. He has profound knowledge and wisdom; he is skilled in discriminating the right path and the wrong path; he has reached the highest goal. He is friendly amidst the hostile, peaceful amidst the violent, and unattached amidst the attached.

In this very life the arahat has realized the end of suffering, laying down the burden of the five aggregates. He has transcended the ties of both merit and demerit; he is sorrowless, stainless, and pure; he is free from attachment and has plunged into the Deathless. Like the moon he is spotless and pure, serene and clear. He has cast off all human bonds and transcended all celestial bonds; he has gotten rid of the substrata of existence and conquered all worlds. He knows the death and rebirth of beings; he is totally detached, blessed and enlightened. No gods, angels, or human beings can find his tracks, for he clings to nothing, has no attachment, holds to nothing. He has reached the end of births, attained the perfection of insight, and reached the summit of spiritual excellence. Bearing his last body, perfectly at peace, the arahat is the living demonstration of the truth of the Dhamma. By his own example he shows that it is possible to free oneself from the stains of greed, hatred, and delusion, to rise above suffering, and to win Nibbāna in this very life.

The arahat ideal reaches its optimal exemplification in the Buddha, the promulgator and master of the entire teaching. It was the Buddha who, without any aid or guidance, rediscovered the ancient path to deliverance and taught it to countless others. His arising in the world provides the precious opportunity to hear and practise the excellent Dhamma (182, 194). He is the giver and shower of refuge (190–192), the Supreme Teacher who depends on nothing but his own self-evolved wisdom (353). Born a man, the Buddha always remains essentially human, yet his attainment of Perfect Enlightenment elevates him to a level far surpassing that of common humanity. All our familiar concepts and modes of knowing fail to circumscribe his nature: he is trackless, of limitless range, free from all worldliness, the conqueror of all, the knower of all, untainted by the world (179, 180, 353). Always shining in the splendour of his wisdom, the Buddha by his very being confirms the Buddhist faith in human perfectibility and consummates the Dhammapada's picture of the fully accomplished individual, the arahat.

* * *

The four levels of teaching just discussed give us the key for sorting out the Dhammapada's diverse utterances on Buddhist doctrine and for discerning the intention behind its words of practical counsel. Interlaced with the verses specific to these four main levels, there runs throughout the work a large number of verses not tied to any single level but applicable to all alike. Taken together, these delineate for us the basic world view of early Buddhism. The most arresting feature of this view is its stress on process rather than persistence as the defining mark of actuality. The universe is in flux, a boundless river of incessant becoming sweeping everything along; dust motes and mountains, gods and human beings and animals, world system after world system without number—all are engulfed by the irrepressible current. There is no creator of this process, no providential deity behind the scenes steering all things to some great and glorious end. The cosmos is beginningless, and in its movement from phase to phase it is governed only by the impersonal, implacable law of arising, change, and passing away.

However, the focus of the Dhammapada is not on the outer cosmos, but on the human world, upon man with his yearning and his suffering, his immense complexity, his striving and movement towards transcendence. The starting point is the human condition as given, and fundamental to the picture that emerges is the inescapable duality of human life, the dichotomies which taunt and challenge us at every turn. Seeking happiness, afraid of pain, loss, and death, we walk the delicate balance between good and evil, purity and defilement, progress and decline. Our actions are strung out between these moral antipodes, and because we cannot evade the necessity to choose, we must bear the full responsibility for our decisions. Our moral freedom is a reason for both dread and jubilation, for by means of our choices we determine our own individual destiny, not only through one life, but through the numerous lives to be turned up by the rolling wheel of saṃsāra. If we choose wrongly we can sink to the lowest depths of degradation; if we choose rightly we can make ourselves worthy even of the homage of the gods. The paths to all destinations branch out from the present, from the ineluctable immediate occasion of conscious choice and action.

The recognition of duality extends beyond the limits of conditioned existence to include the antithetical poles of the conditioned and the unconditioned, saṃsāra and Nibbāna, the "near shore" and the "far shore." The Buddha appears in the world as the Great Liberator who shows us the way to break free from the one and arrive at the other, where alone true safety is to be found. But all he can do is indicate the path; the work of treading it lies with the disciple. The Dhammapada again and again sounds this challenge to human freedom: man is the maker and master of himself, the protector or destroyer of himself, the saviour of himself (160, 165, 380). In the end we must choose between the way that leads back into the world, to the round of becoming, and the way that leads out of the world, to Nibbāna. And though this last course is extremely difficult and demanding, the voice of the Buddha speaks words of assurance confirming that it can be done, that it lies within our power to overcome all barriers and to triumph even over death itself.

The pivotal role in achieving progress in all spheres, the Dhammapada declares, is played by the mind. In contrast to the Bible, which opens with an account of God's creation of the world, the Dhammapada begins with a bold assertion that mind is the forerunner of all that we are, the maker of our character, the creator of our destiny. The entire discipline of the Buddha, from basic morality to the highest levels of meditation, hinges upon training the mind. A wrongly directed mind brings greater harm than any enemy, a rightly directed mind brings greater good than any other relative or friend (42–43). The mind is unruly, fickle, difficult to subdue, but by effort, mindfulness, and unflagging self-discipline, one can master its vagrant tendencies, escape the torrents of the passions, and find "an island which no flood can overwhelm" (25). The one who conquers himself, the victor over his own mind, achieves a conquest which can never be undone, a victory greater than that of the mightiest warriors (103–105).

What is needed most urgently to train and subdue the mind is a quality called heedfulness (*appamāda*). Heedfulness combines critical self-awareness and unremitting energy in the task of keeping the mind under constant observation to detect and expel the defiling impulses whenever they seek an opportunity to surface. In a world where we have no saviour but ourselves, and where the means to deliverance lies in mental purification, heedfulness becomes the crucial factor for ensuring that we keep to the straight path of training without deviating due to the seductive allurements of sense pleasures or the stagnating influences of laziness and complacency. Heedfulness, the Buddha declares, is the path to the Deathless; heedlessness, the path to death. The wise who understand this distinction abide in heedfulness and experience Nibbāna, "the incomparable freedom from bondage" (21–23).

As a great religious classic and the chief spiritual testament of early Buddhism, the Dhammapada cannot be gauged in its true value by a single reading, even if that reading is done carefully and reverentially. It yields its riches only through repeated study, sustained reflection, and most importantly, through the application of its principles to daily life. Thus it might be suggested to the reader in search of spiritual guidance that the Dhammapada be used as a manual for contemplation. After an initial reading, one would do well to read several verses or even a whole chapter every day, slowly and carefully, relishing the words. One should reflect on the meaning of each verse deeply and thoroughly, investigate its relevance to one's life, and apply it as a guide to conduct. If this is done repeatedly, with patience and perseverance, it is certain that the Dhammapada will confer upon one's life a new meaning and sense of purpose. Infusing one with hope and inspiration, gradually it will lead one to discover a freedom and happiness far greater than anything the world can offer.

Bhikkhu Bodhi

The Dhammapada

Namo Tassa Bhagavato Arahato Sammāsambuddhassa
Homage to Him, the Blessed One, the Perfected One,
the Supremely Enlightened One!

1

Yamakavagga
The Pairs

1. Manopubbaṅgamā dhammā manoseṭṭhā manomayā;
manasā ce paduṭṭhena bhāsati vā karoti vā
tato naṃ dukkham anveti cakkaṃ va vahato padaṃ.

1. Mind precedes all mental states. Mind is their chief; they are all mind-wrought. If with an impure mind a person speaks or acts, suffering follows him like the wheel that follows the foot of the ox. [1]

2. Manopubbaṅgamā dhammā manoseṭṭhā manomayā;
manasā ce pasannena bhāsati vā karoti vā
tato naṃ sukham anveti chāyā va anapāyinī.

2. Mind precedes all mental states. Mind is their chief; they are all mind-wrought. If with a pure mind a person speaks or acts, happiness follows him like his never-departing shadow. [2]

3. "Akkocchi maṃ, avadhi maṃ, ajini maṃ, ahāsi me,"
ye ca taṃ upanayhanti, veraṃ tesaṃ na sammati.

3. "He abused me, he struck me, he overpowered me, he robbed me"—those who harbour such thoughts do not still their hatred. [3]

4. "Akkocchi maṃ, avadhi maṃ, ajini maṃ, ahāsi me,"
ye ca taṃ n'upanayhanti, veraṃ tes'ūpasammati.

4. "He abused me, he struck me, he overpowered me, he robbed me"—those who do not harbour such thoughts still their hatred. [4]

5. *Na hi verena verāni sammant'īdha kudācanaṃ,*
averena ca sammanti: esa dhammo sanantano.

5. Hatred is never appeased by hatred in this world; by non-hatred alone is hatred appeased. This is an eternal law. [5]

6. *Pare ca na vijānanti, mayam ettha yamāmase;*
ye ca tattha vijānanti, tato sammanti medhagā.

6. There are those who do not realize that one day we all must die, but those who realize this settle their quarrels. [6]

7. *Subhānupassiṃ viharantaṃ indriyesu asaṃvutaṃ*
bhojanamhi cāmattaññuṃ kusītaṃ hīnavīriyaṃ,
taṃ ve pasahati Māro vāto rukkhaṃ va dubbalaṃ.

7. Just as a storm throws down a weak tree, so does Māra overpower one who lives for the pursuit of pleasures, who is uncontrolled in his senses, immoderate in eating, indolent and dissipated.[1] [7]

8. *Asubhānupassiṃ viharantaṃ indriyesu susaṃvutaṃ*
bhojanamhi ca mattaññuṃ saddhaṃ āraddhavīriyaṃ,
taṃ ve nappasahati Māro vāto selaṃ va pabbataṃ.

8. Just as a storm cannot throw down a rocky mountain, so Māra can never overpower one who lives meditating on the impurities, who is controlled in his senses, moderate in eating, and filled with faith and earnest effort.[2] [8]

9. *Anikkasāvo kāsāvaṃ yo vatthaṃ paridahissati*
apeto damasaccena, na so kāsāvam arahati.

---

1. Māra: the Tempter in Buddhism, represented in the scriptures as an evil-minded deity who tries to lead people away from the path to liberation. The commentaries explain Māra as the lord of evil forces, as mental defilements, and as death.
2. The impurities (*asubha*): subjects of meditation which focus on the inherent repulsiveness of the body, recommended especially as powerful antidotes to lust.

9. Whoever wears the monk's yellow robe while being depraved, devoid of self-control and truthfulness, he surely is not worthy of the yellow robe. [9]

> *10. Yo ca vantakasāv'assa sīlesu susamāhito*
> *upeto damasaccena, sa ve kāsāvam arahati.*

10. But whoever is purged of depravity, well established in virtues, and filled with self-control and truthfulness, he indeed is worthy of the yellow robe. [10]

> *11. Asāre sāramatino sāre cāsāradassino,*
> *te sāraṃ nādhigacchanti micchāsaṅkappagocarā.*

11. Those who mistake the unessential to be essential and the essential to be unessential, dwelling in wrong thoughts, never arrive at the essential. [11]

> *12. Sārañ ca sārato ñatvā asārañ ca asārato,*
> *te sāram adhigacchanti sammāsaṅkappagocarā.*

12. Those who know the essential to be essential and the unessential to be unessential, dwelling in right thoughts, arrive at the essential. [12]

> *13. Yathā agāraṃ ducchannaṃ vuṭṭhi samativijjhati,*
> *evaṃ abhāvitaṃ cittaṃ rāgo samativijjhati.*

13. Just as the rain breaks through an ill-thatched house, even so passion penetrates an undeveloped mind. [13]

> *14. Yathā agāraṃ succhannaṃ vuṭṭhi na samativijjhati,*
> *evaṃ subhāvitaṃ cittaṃ rāgo na samativijjhati.*

14. Just as the rain does not break through a well-thatched house, even so passion never penetrates a well-developed mind. [14]

> *15. Idha socati pecca socati, pāpakārī ubhayattha socati;*
> *so socati so vihaññati, disvā kammakiliṭṭham attano.*

15. The evil-doer grieves here, he grieves hereafter; he grieves in both worlds. He laments and is afflicted, recollecting his own impure deeds. [15]

16. Idha modati pecca modati, katapuñño ubhayattha modati;
so modati so pamodati, disvā kammavisuddhim attano.

16. The doer of good rejoices here, he rejoices hereafter; he rejoices in both worlds. He rejoices and exults, recollecting his own pure deeds. [16]

17. Idha tappati pecca tappati, pāpakārī ubhayattha tappati;
pāpaṃ me katan ti tappati, bhiyyo tappati duggatiṃ gato.

17. The evil-doer suffers here, he suffers hereafter; he suffers in both worlds. The thought, "Evil have I done," torments him, and he suffers even more when gone to realms of woe. [17]

18. Idha nandati pecca nandati, katapuñño ubhayattha nandati;
puññaṃ me katan ti nandati, bhiyyo nandati suggatiṃ gato.

18. The doer of good delights here, he delights hereafter; he delights in both worlds. The thought, "Good have I done," delights him, and he delights even more when gone to realms of bliss. [18]

19. Bahum pi ce sahitaṃ bhāsamāno na takkaro hoti naro pamatto
gopo va gāvo gaṇayaṃ paresaṃ na bhāgavā sāmaññassa hoti.

19. Although he recites many sacred texts, if he does not act accordingly, that heedless man is like a cowherd who only counts the cattle of others—he does not partake of the blessings of a holy life. [19]

20. *Appam pi ce sahitaṃ bhāsamāno dhammassa hoti anudhammacārī*
rāgañ ca dosañ ca pahāya mohaṃ sammappajāno suvimuttacitto
anupādiyāno idha vā huraṃ vā, sa bhāgavā sāmaññassa hoti.

20. Although he recites few sacred texts, if he puts the Dhamma into practice, forsaking lust, hatred, and delusion, with true wisdom and emancipated mind, clinging to nothing in this or any other world—he, indeed, partakes of the blessings of a holy life. [20]

2

Appamādavagga

Heedfulness

21. Appamādo amatapadaṃ, pamādo maccuno padaṃ;
appamattā na mīyanti, ye pamattā yathā matā.

21. Heedfulness is the path to the Deathless, heedlessness is the path to death. The heedful do not die, the heedless are already dead.[3] [1]

22. Etaṃ visesato ñatvā appamādamhi paṇḍitā,
appamāde pamodanti ariyānaṃ gocare ratā.

22. Clearly understanding this excellence of heedfulness, the wise exult therein and enjoy the resort of the noble ones.[4] [2]

23. Te jhāyino sātatikā niccaṃ daḷhaparakkamā,
phusanti dhīrā nibbānaṃ yogakkhemaṃ anuttaraṃ.

23. The wise ones, ever meditative and steadfastly persevering, experience Nibbāna, the incomparable freedom from bondage. [3]

24. Uṭṭhānavato satimato sucikammassa nisammakārino
saññatassa ca dhammajīvino appamattassa yaso'
bhivaḍḍhati.

24. Ever grows the glory of one who is energetic, mindful, and pure in conduct, discerning and self-controlled, righteous and heedful. [4]

---

3. The Deathless (*amata*): Nibbāna, so called because those who attain it are freed from the cycle of repeated birth and death.
4. The noble ones (*ariya*): those who have reached any of the four stages of supramundane attainment leading irreversibly to Nibbāna. See Introduction, pp.13–15.

25. *Uṭṭhānen'appamādena saññamena damena ca*
dīpaṃ kayirātha medhāvī yaṃ ogho nābhikīrati.

25. By effort and heedfulness, discipline and self-mastery, let the wise one make for himself an island which no flood can overwhelm. [5]

26. *Pamādam anuyuñjanti bālā dummedhino janā,*
appamādañ ca medhāvī dhanaṃ seṭṭhaṃ va rakkhati.

26. The foolish and ignorant indulge in heedlessness, but the wise one guards heedfulness as his best treasure. [6]

27. *Mā pamādam anuyuñjetha, mā kāmaratisanthavaṃ;*
appamatto hi jhāyanto pappoti vipulaṃ sukhaṃ.

27. Do not give way to heedlessness; do not indulge in sensual pleasures. Only the heedful and meditative attain great happiness. [7]

28. *Pamādaṃ appamādena yadā nudati paṇḍito,*
paññāpāsādam āruyha asoko sokiniṃ pajaṃ,
pabbataṭṭho va bhummaṭṭhe, dhīro bāle avekkhati.

28. Just as one upon the summit of a mountain beholds the groundlings, even so when the wise man casts away heedlessness by heedfulness and ascends the high tower of wisdom, this sorrowless sage beholds the sorrowing and foolish -multitude. [8]

29. *Appamatto pamattesu suttesu bahujāgaro*
abalassaṃ va sīghasso hitvā yāti sumedhaso.

29. Heedful among the heedless, wide awake among the sleepy, the wise man advances like a swift horse leaving behind a weak nag. [9]

30. *Appamādena Maghavā devānaṃ seṭṭhataṃ gato;*
appamādaṃ pasaṃsanti pamādo garahito sadā.

30. By heedfulness did Indra become the overlord of the gods. Heedfulness is ever praised, and heedlessness ever despised.[5] [10]

31. Appamādarato bhikkhu pamāde bhayadassivā
saññojanaṃ aṇuṃ thūlaṃ ḍahaṃ aggī va gacchati.

31. The monk who delights in heedfulness and looks with fear at heedlessness advances like fire, burning all fetters subtle and coarse. [11]

32. Appamādarato bhikkhu pamāde bhayadassivā
abhabbo parihānāya, nibbānass'eva santike.

32. The monk who delights in heedfulness and looks with fear at heedlessness will not fall. He is close to Nibbāna. [12]

5. Indra: the ruler of the gods in ancient Indian mythology.

3

Cittavagga
The Mind

33. Phandanaṃ capalaṃ cittaṃ durakkhaṃ dunnivārayaṃ
ujuṃ karoti medhāvī usukāro va tejanaṃ.

33. Just as an arrow-maker straightens an arrow shaft, even so the discerning person straightens his mind—so fickle and unsteady, so difficult to guard and control. [1]

34. Vārijo va thale khitto okamokata ubbhato,
pariphandat'idaṃ cittaṃ Māradheyyaṃ pahātave.

34. As a fish when pulled out of water and cast on land throbs and quivers, even so is this mind agitated. Hence one should leave the realm of Māra. [2]

35. Dunniggahassa lahuno yatthakāmanipātino
cittassa damatho sādhu: cittaṃ dantaṃ sukhāvahaṃ.

35. Wonderful, indeed, it is to subdue the mind, so difficult to subdue, ever swift, and wandering wherever it desires. A tamed mind brings happiness. [3]

36. Sududdasaṃ sunipuṇaṃ yatthakāmanipātinaṃ
cittaṃ rakkhetha medhāvī: cittaṃ guttaṃ sukhāvahaṃ.

36. Let the discerning person guard his mind, so difficult to detect and extremely subtle, wandering wherever it desires. A guarded mind brings happiness. [4]

37. Dūraṅgamaṃ ekacaraṃ asarīraṃ guhāsayaṃ
ye cittaṃ saññamessanti mokkhanti Mārabandhanā.

37. Dwelling in the cave (of the heart), without form, the mind wanders far and moves alone. Those who subdue this mind are liberated from the bonds of Māra. [5]

38. Anavaṭṭhitacittassa saddhammaṃ avijānato
pariplavapasādassa paññā na paripūrati.

38. Wisdom is not perfected in one whose mind is not steadfast, who knows not the Good Teaching, and whose faith wavers. [6]

39. Anavassutacittassa ananvāhatacetaso
puññapāpapahīnassa natthi jāgarato bhayaṃ.

39. There is no fear for an Awakened One, whose mind is not sodden (by lust) nor afflicted (by hate), and who has gone beyond both merit and demerit.[6] [7]

40. Kumbhūpamaṃ kāyam imaṃ viditvā, nagarūpamaṃ cittam idaṃ ṭhapetvā,
yodhetha Māraṃ paññāvudhena, jitañ ca rakkhe anivesano siyā.

40. Realizing that this body is as fragile as a clay pot, and fortifying this mind like a well-fortified city, fight out Māra with the sword of wisdom. Then, guarding the conquest, remain unattached. [8]

41. Aciraṃ vat'ayaṃ kāyo paṭhaviṃ adhisessati
chuddho apetaviññāṇo niratthaṃ va kaliṅgaraṃ.

41. Before long, alas, this body will lie upon the earth, cast away and lifeless, like a useless log. [9]

42. Diso disaṃ yaṃ taṃ kayirā verī vā pana verinaṃ,
micchāpaṇihitaṃ cittaṃ pāpiyo naṃ tato kare.

42. Whatever harm an enemy may do to an enemy, or a hater to a hater, an ill-directed mind inflicts on oneself greater harm. [10]

---

6. The arahat is said to be beyond both merit and demerit because, as he has abandoned all defilements, he can no longer perform evil actions; and as he has no more attachment, his virtuous actions no longer bear kammic fruit.

43. *Na taṃ mātā pitā kayirā aññe vāpi ca ñātakā,*
sammāpaṇihitaṃ cittaṃ seyyaso naṃ tato kare.

43. Neither mother, father, nor any other relative can do one greater good than one's own well-directed mind. [11]

4

Pupphavagga

Flowers

44. *Ko imaṃ paṭhaviṃ vijessati Yamalokañ ca imaṃ sadevakaṃ?*
ko dhammapadaṃ sudesitaṃ kusalo puppham iva pacessati?

44. Who shall overcome this earth, the world of misery, and this sphere of humans and gods? Who shall bring to -perfection the well-taught path of wisdom as an expert garland-maker would his floral design? [1]

45. *Sekho paṭhaviṃ vijessati Yamalokañ ca imaṃ sadevakaṃ,*
sekho dhammapadaṃ sudesitaṃ kusalo puppham iva pacessati.

45. A striver-on-the-path shall overcome this earth, the world of misery, and this sphere of humans and gods. The striver-on-the-path shall bring to perfection the well-taught path of wisdom, as an expert garland-maker would his floral design.[7] [2]

46. *Pheṇūpamaṃ kāyam imaṃ viditvā marīcidhammaṃ abhisambudhāno*
chetvāna Mārassa papupphakāni adassanaṃ Maccurājassa gacche.

46. Realizing that this body is like froth, penetrating its mirage-like nature, and plucking out Māra's flower-tipped arrows (of sensuality), go beyond sight of the King of Death! [3]

---

7. The striver-on-the-path (*sekha*): one who has achieved any of the first three stages of supramundane attainment: a stream-enterer, once-returner, or non-returner.

> 47. *Pupphāni h'eva pacinantaṃ byāsattamanasaṃ naraṃ*
> *suttaṃ gāmaṃ mahogho va maccu ādāya gacchati.*

47. As a mighty flood sweeps away the sleeping village, so Death carries away the person of grasping mind who only collects the flowers (of pleasure). [4]

> 48. *Pupphāni h'eva pacinantaṃ byāsattamanasaṃ naraṃ*
> *atittaṃ yeva kāmesu antako kurute vasaṃ.*

48. The Destroyer brings under his sway the person of grasping mind who, insatiate in sense desires, only collects the flowers (of pleasure). [5]

> 49. *Yathāpi bhamaro pupphaṃ vaṇṇagandhaṃ aheṭhayaṃ*
> *paleti rasam ādāya evaṃ game munī care.*

49. As a bee gathers honey from the flower without injuring its colour or fragrance, even so the sage should go on his alms round in the village.[8] [6]

> 50. *Na paresaṃ vilomāni na paresaṃ katākataṃ*
> *attano va avekkheyya katāni akatāni ca.*

50. Let none find fault with others; let none see the omissions and commissions of others. But let one see one's own acts, done and undone. [7]

> 51. *Yathāpi ruciraṃ pupphaṃ vaṇṇavantaṃ agandhakaṃ,*
> *evaṃ subhāsitā vācā aphalā hoti akubbato.*

51. Like a beautiful flower full of colour but without fragrance, even so, fruitless are the fair words of one who does not practise them. [8]

> 52. *Yathāpi ruciraṃ pupphaṃ vaṇṇavantaṃ sagandhakaṃ,*
> *evaṃ subhāsitā vācā saphalā hoti sakubbato.*

---

8. The "sage in the village" is the Buddhist monk who receives his food by going silently from door to door with his almsbowl, accepting whatever is offered.

52. Like a beautiful flower full of colour and also fragrant, even so, fruitful are the fair words of one who practises them. [9]

> 53. *Yathāpi puppharāsimhā kayirā mālāguṇe bahū,*
> *evaṃ jātena maccena kattabbaṃ kusalaṃ bahuṃ.*

53. As from a great heap of flowers many garlands can be made, even so should many good deeds be done by one born a mortal. [10]

> 54. *Na pupphagandho paṭivātam eti, na candanaṃ tagaramallikā vā,*
> *satañ ca gandho paṭivātam eti; sabbā disā sappuriso pavāti.*

54. Not the sweet smell of flowers, not even the fragrance of sandal, *tagara*, or jasmine goes against the wind. But the fragrance of the virtuous goes against the wind. The virtuous person pervades all directions with the fragrance of virtue.[9] [11]

> 55. *Candanaṃ tagaraṃ vāpi uppalaṃ atha vassikī,*
> *etesaṃ gandhajātānaṃ sīlagandho anuttaro.*

55. Of all the fragrances—sandal, *tagara*, blue lotus, and jasmine—the fragrance of virtue is by far the sweetest. [12]

> 56. *Appamatto ayaṃ gandho yāyaṃ tagaracandanī,*
> *yo ca sīlavataṃ gandho vāti devesu uttamo.*

56. Faint is the fragrance of *tagara* and sandal, but the fragrance of the virtuous is excellent, wafting even among the gods. [13]

> 57. *Tesaṃ sampannasīlānaṃ appamādavihārinaṃ*
> *sammadaññā vimuttānaṃ Māro maggaṃ na vindati.*

57. Māra never finds the path of the truly virtuous, who abide in vigilance and are freed by perfect knowledge. [14]

---

9. *Tagara:* a fragrant powder obtained from a particular kind of shrub.

58. *Yathā saṅkāradhānasmiṃ ujjhitasmiṃ mahāpathe*
padumaṃ tattha jāyetha sucigandhaṃ manoramaṃ.

59. *Evaṃ saṅkārabhūtesu andhabhūte puthujjane*
atirocati paññ'ya Sammāsambuddhasāvako.

58–59. As upon a heap of rubbish in the roadside ditch blooms a lotus, fragrant and pleasing, even so, on the rubbish heap of blind worldlings the disciple of the Supremely Enlightened One shines resplendent in wisdom. [15-16]

5

Bālavagga
The Fool

60. *Dīghā jāgarato ratti, dīghaṃ santassa yojanaṃ,*
dīgho bālānaṃ saṃsāro saddhammaṃ avijānataṃ.

60. Long is the night to the sleepless; long is the league to the weary; long is worldly existence to fools who know not the Good Teaching. [1]

61. *Carañ ce nādhigaccheyya seyyaṃ sadisam attano,*
ekacariyaṃ daḷhaṃ kayirā: natthi bāle sahāyatā.

61. Should a seeker not find a companion who is his better or equal, let him resolutely pursue a solitary course; there is no fellowship with a fool. [2]

62. *"Puttā m'atthi dhanam m'atthi," iti bālo vihaññati,*
attā hi attano natthi kuto puttā kuto dhanaṃ?

62. The fool worries, thinking, "I have sons, I have wealth." Indeed, when he himself is not his own, whence are sons, whence is wealth? [3]

63. *Yo bālo maññati bālyaṃ, paṇḍito vāpi tena so,*
bālo ca paṇḍitamānī sa ve bālo ti vuccati.

63. A fool who knows his foolishness is wise at least to that extent, but a fool who thinks himself wise is called a fool indeed. [4]

64. *Yāvajīvam pi ce bālo paṇḍitaṃ payirupāsati,*
na so dhammaṃ vijānāti dabbī sūparasaṃ yathā.

64. Though all his life a fool associate with a wise man, he no more comprehends the Dhamma than a spoon tastes the flavour of the soup. [5]

65. Muhuttam api ce viññū paṇḍitaṃ payirupāsati,
khippaṃ dhammaṃ vijānāti jivhā sūparasaṃ yathā.

65. Though only for a moment a discerning person associate with a wise man, quickly he comprehends the Dhamma, just as the tongue tastes the flavour of the soup. [6]

66. Caranti bālā dummedhā amitten'eva attanā
karontā pāpakaṃ kammaṃ yaṃ hoti kaṭukapphalaṃ.

66. Fools of little wit are enemies unto themselves as they move about doing evil deeds, the fruits of which are bitter. [7]

67. Na taṃ kammaṃ kataṃ sādhu yaṃ katvā anutappati,
yassa assumukho rodaṃ vipākaṃ paṭisevati.

67. Ill done is that action which, having been done, is repented later, and the fruits of which one reaps weeping with a tearful face. [8]

68. Tañ ca kammaṃ kataṃ sādhu yaṃ katvā nānutappati,
yassa patīto sumano vipākaṃ paṭisevati.

68. Well done is that action which, having been done, is not repented later, and the fruits of which one reaps with delight and happiness. [9]

69. Madhu va maññatī bālo yāva pāpaṃ na paccati,
yadā ca paccati pāpaṃ atha bālo dukkhaṃ nigacchati.

69. So long as an evil deed has not ripened, the fool thinks it as sweet as honey. But when the evil deed ripens, the fool comes to grief. [10]

70. Māse māse kusaggena bālo bhuñjetha bhojanaṃ,
na so saṅkhātadhammānaṃ kalaṃ agghati soḷasiṃ.

70. Month after month a fool may eat his food with the tip of a blade of grass, but he still is not worth a sixteenth part of those who have comprehended the Dhamma. [11]

71. Na hi pāpaṃ kataṃ kammaṃ sajju khīraṃ va muccati,
ḍahantaṃ bālam anveti bhasmacchanno va pāvako.

71. Truly, an evil deed committed does not immediately bear fruit, like milk that does not turn sour all at once. But smouldering, it follows the fool like fire covered by ashes. [12]

72. Yāvadeva anatthāya ñattaṃ bālassa jāyati,
hanti bālassa sukkaṃsaṃ muddham assa vipātayaṃ.

72. To his own ruin the fool gains knowledge, for it cleaves his head and destroys his innate goodness. [13]

73. Asantaṃ bhāvanam iccheyya, purekkhārañ ca bhikkhusu,
āvāsesu ca issariyaṃ, pūjaṃ parakulesu ca.

73. The fool seeks undeserved reputation, precedence among monks, authority over monasteries, and honour among householders. [14]

74. "Mam'eva katam maññantu gihī pabbajitā ubho,
mam'ev'ātivasā assu kiccākiccesu kismici,"
iti bālassa saṅkappo icchā māno ca vaḍḍhati.

74. "Let both laymen and monks think that it was done by me. In every work, great and small, let them follow me"—such is the ambition of the fool; thus his desire and pride increase. [15]

75. Aññā hi lābhūpanisā aññā nibbānagāminī,
evam etaṃ abhiññāya bhikkhu Buddhassa sāvako
sakkāraṃ nābhinandeyya vivekam anubrūhaye.

75. One is the quest for worldly gain, and quite another is the path to Nibbāna. Clearly understanding this, let not the monk, the disciple of the Buddha, be carried away by worldly acclaim, but develop detachment instead. [16]

6

Paṇḍitavagga

The Wise Man

76. *Nidhīnaṃ va pavattāraṃ yaṃ passe vajjadassinaṃ,*
niggayhavādiṃ medhāviṃ tādisaṃ paṇḍitaṃ bhaje;
tādisaṃ bhajamānassa seyyo hoti na pāpiyo.

76. If one finds someone who points out faults and who reproves, one should follow such a wise and sagacious person as one would a guide to hidden treasure. It is always better, and never worse, to cultivate such an association. [1]

77. *Ovadeyy'ānusāseyya, asabbhā ca nivāraye,*
sataṃ hi so piyo hoti, asataṃ hoti appiyo.

77. Let him admonish, instruct, and shield one from wrong; he, indeed, is dear to the good and detestable to the evil. [2]

78. *Na bhaje pāpake mitte, na bhaje purisādhame,*
bhajetha mitte kalyāṇe, bhajetha purisuttame.

78. Do not associate with evil companions; do not seek the fellowship of the vile. Associate with good friends; seek the fellowship of noble persons. [3]

79. *Dhammapīti sukhaṃ seti vippasannena cetasā,*
ariyappavedite dhamme sadā ramati paṇḍito.

79. One who drinks deep the Dhamma lives happily with a tranquil mind. The wise person ever delights in the Dhamma made known by the Noble One (the Buddha). [4]

80. *Udakaṃ hi nayanti nettikā, usukārā namayanti tejanaṃ,*
dāruṃ namayanti tacchakā, attānaṃ damayanti paṇḍitā.

80. Irrigators regulate the waters; arrow-makers straighten the arrow shaft; carpenters shape the wood; the wise control themselves. [5]

> *81. Selo yathā ekaghano vātena na samīrati,*
> *evaṃ nindāpasaṃsāsu na samiñjanti paṇḍitā.*

81. Just as a solid rock is not shaken by the wind, even so the wise are not affected by praise or blame. [6]

> *82. Yathāpi rahado gambhīro vippasanno anāvilo,*
> *evaṃ dhammāni sutvāna vippasīdanti paṇḍitā.*

82. On hearing the teachings, the wise become perfectly purified like a lake deep, clear, and limpid. [7]

> *83. Sabbattha ve sappurisā cajanti; na kāmakāmā lapayanti santo.*
> *Sukhena phuṭṭhā atha vā dukhena n'uccāvacaṃ paṇḍitā dassayanti.*

83. The good renounce (attachment for) everything; the virtuous do not prattle with a yearning for pleasures. The wise show no elation or depression when touched by happiness or sorrow. [8]

> *84. Na attahetu na parassa hetu, na puttam icche na dhanaṃ na raṭṭhaṃ,*
> *na iccheyya adhammena samiddhim attano, sa sīlavā paññavā dhammiko siyā.*

84. He is truly virtuous, wise, and righteous, who neither for his own sake nor for the sake of another (does any wrong), who does not crave for sons, wealth, or kingdom, and does not desire his own success by unjust means. [9]

> *85. Appakā te manussesu ye janā pāragāmino,*
> *ath'āyaṃ itarā pajā tīram ev'ānudhāvati.*

85. Few among human beings are those who cross to the farther shore. The rest, the bulk of people, only run up and down the hither bank. [10]

86. Ye ca kho sammadakkhāte dhamme dhammānuvattino,
te janā pāram essanti maccudheyyaṃ suduttaraṃ.

86. But those people who act according to the perfectly taught Dhamma will cross the realm of Death, so difficult to cross. [11]

87. Kaṇhaṃ dhammaṃ vippahāya sukkaṃ bhāvetha paṇḍito,
okā anokaṃ āgamma viveke yattha dūramaṃ.

88. Tatrābhiratim iccheyya hitvā kāme akiñcano,
pariyodapeyya attānaṃ cittaklesehi paṇḍito.

87–88. Abandoning the dark way, let the wise man cultivate the bright path. Having gone from home to homelessness, let him yearn for that delight in detachment, so difficult to enjoy. Giving up sensual pleasures, with no attachment, the wise man should cleanse himself of defilements of the mind.[12-13]

89. Yesaṃ sambodhi-aṅgesu sammā cittaṃ subhāvitaṃ,
ādānapaṭinissagge anupādāya ye ratā,
khīṇāsavā jutīmanto te loke parinibbutā.

89. Those whose minds have reached full excellence in the factors of enlightenment, who, having renounced acquisitiveness, rejoice in not clinging to things—rid of cankers, glowing with wisdom, they have attained Nibbāna in this very life.[10] [14]

---

10. This verse describes the arahat, dealt with more fully in the following chapter. The "cankers" (*āsava*) are the four basic defilements of sensual desire, desire for continued existence, false views, and ignorance.

7

Arahantavagga

The Arahat or Perfected One

90. Gataddhino visokassa vippamuttassa sabbadhi
sabbaganthappahīnassa pariḷāho na vijjati.

90. The fever of passion does not exist for one who has completed the journey, who is sorrowless and wholly set free, and has broken all ties. [1]

91. Uyyuñjanti satīmanto, na nikete ramanti te,
haṃsā va pallalaṃ hitvā okamokaṃ jahanti te.

91. The mindful ones exert themselves. They are not attached to any home; like swans that abandon the lake, they leave home after home behind. [2]

92. Yesaṃ sannicayo natthi, ye pariññātabhojanā,
suññato animitto ca vimokkho yesaṃ gocaro,
ākāse va sakuntānaṃ gati tesaṃ durannayā.

92. Those who do not accumulate and are wise regarding food, whose object is the Void, the unconditioned freedom—their track, like that of birds in the air, cannot be traced. [3]

93. Yass'āsavā parikkhīṇā āhāre ca anissito,
suññato animitto ca vimokkho yassa gocaro,
ākāse va sakuntānaṃ padaṃ tassa durannayaṃ.

93. He whose cankers are destroyed and who is not attached to food, whose object is the Void, the unconditioned freedom—his path, like that of birds in the air, cannot be traced. [4]

94. Yass'indriyāni samathaṅgatāni, assā yathā sārathinā sudantā,
pahīnamānassa anāsavassa devā pi tassa pihayanti tādino.

94. Even the gods hold dear the steadfast one, whose senses are subdued like horses well trained by a charioteer, whose pride is destroyed, and who is free from the cankers. [5]

95. Paṭhavīsamo no virujjhati, indakhīlūpamo tādi subbato,
rahado va apetakaddamo, saṃsārā na bhavanti tādino.

95. There is no more worldly existence for the steadfast one, who, like the earth, resents nothing; who is as firm as a high pillar and as pure as a deep pool free from mud. [6]

96. Santaṃ tassa manaṃ hoti santā vācā ca kamma ca,
sammadaññā vimuttassa upasantassa tādino.

96. Calm is his thought, calm his speech, and calm his deed, who, truly knowing, is wholly freed, perfectly tranquil, and steadfast. [7]

97. Assaddho akataññū ca sandhicchedo ca yo naro,
hatāvakāso vantāso sa ve uttamaporiso.

97. The man who is without blind faith, who knows the Uncreate, who has severed all links, who has destroyed all causes (for kamma, good and evil), and who has thrown out all desires—he truly is the most excellent of men.[11] [8]

98. Gāme vā yadi vā'raññe ninne vā yadī vā thale,
yatth'ārahanto viharanti taṃ bhūmiṃ rāmaṇeyyakaṃ.

98. Inspiring, indeed, is that place where arahats dwell, be it a village, a forest, a vale, or a hill. [9]

99. Ramaṇīyāni araññāni, yattha na ramatī jano,
vītarāgā ramissanti, na te kāmagavesino.

99. Inspiring are the forests where worldlings find no pleasure. There the passionless will rejoice, for they seek no sensual pleasures. [10]

---

11. In the Pāli this verse presents a series of puns, and if the "underside" of each pun were to be translated, the verse would read thus: "The man who is faithless, ungrateful, a burglar, who destroys opportunities and eats vomit—he truly is the most excellent of men."

8

Sahassavagga
The Thousands

100. Sahassam api ce vācā anatthapadasaṃhitā,
ekaṃ atthapadaṃ seyyo yaṃ sutvā upasammati.

100. Better than a thousand meaningless words is one meaningful word, hearing which one attains peace. [11]

101. Sahassam api ce gāthā anatthapadasaṃhitā,
ekaṃ gāthāpadaṃ seyyo yaṃ sutvā upasammati.

101. Better than a thousand meaningless verses is one meaningful verse, hearing which one attains peace. [12]

102. Yo ca gāthāsataṃ bhāse anatthapadasaṃhitā,
ekaṃ dhammapadaṃ seyyo yaṃ sutvā upasammati.

102. Better than reciting a hundred meaningless verses is the reciting of one verse of Dhamma, hearing which one attains peace. [13]

103. Yo sahassaṃ sahassena saṅgāme mānuse jine,
ekañ ca jeyyam attānaṃ sa ve saṅgāmajuttamo.

103. Though one may conquer a thousand times a thousand men in battle, yet he indeed is the noblest victor who conquers himself. [14]

104. Attā have jitaṃ seyyo yā c'āyaṃ itarā pajā,
attadantassa posassa niccaṃ saññatacārino.

105. N'eva devo na gandhabbo, na Māro saha Brahmunā,
jitaṃ apajitaṃ kayirā tathārūpassa jantuno.

104–105. Self-conquest is far better than the conquest of others. Not even a god, an angel, Māra, or Brahmā can turn into defeat the victory of such a person who is self-subdued and ever restrained in conduct.[12] [5-6]

106. Māse māse sahassena yo yajetha sataṃ samaṃ,
ekañ ca bhāvitattānaṃ muhuttam api pūjaye,
sā yeva pūjanā seyyo yañ ce vassasataṃ hutaṃ.

106. Though month after month for a hundred years one should offer sacrifices by the thousands, yet if only for a moment one should worship those of developed mind, that worship is indeed better than a century of sacrifice. [7]

107. Yo ce vassasataṃ jantu aggiṃ paricare vane,
ekañ ca bhāvitattānaṃ muhuttam api pūjaye,
sā yeva pūjanā seyyo yañ ce vassasataṃ hutaṃ.

107. Though for a hundred years one should tend the sacrificial fire in the forest, yet if only for a moment one should worship those of developed mind, that worship is indeed better than a century of sacrifice. [8]

108. Yaṃ kiñci yiṭṭhaṃ va hutaṃ va loke saṃvaccharaṃ yajetha puññapekho,
sabbampi taṃ na catubhāgam eti abhivādanā ujjugatesu seyyo.

108. Whatever gifts and oblations one seeking merit might offer in this world for a whole year, all that is not worth one fourth of the merit gained by revering the upright ones, which is truly excellent. [9]

109. Abhivādanasīlissa niccaṃ vuḍḍhāpacāyino
cattāro dhammā vaḍḍhanti: āyu vaṇṇo sukhaṃ balaṃ.

109. To one ever eager to revere and serve the elders, these four blessings accrue: long life and beauty, happiness and power. [10]

12. Brahmā: a high divinity in ancient Indian religion.

110. Yo ca vassasataṃ jīve dussīlo asamāhito,
ekāhaṃ jīvitaṃ seyyo sīlavantassa jhāyino.

110. Better it is to live one day virtuous and meditative than to live a hundred years immoral and uncontrolled. [11]

111. Yo ca vassasataṃ jīve duppañño asamāhito,
ekāhaṃ jīvitaṃ seyyo paññāvantassa jhāyino.

111. Better it is to live one day wise and meditative than to live a hundred years foolish and uncontrolled. [12]

112. Yo ca vassasataṃ jīve kusīto hīnavīriyo,
ekāhaṃ jīvitaṃ seyyo viriyam ārabhato daḷhaṃ.

112. Better it is to live one day strenuous and resolute than to live a hundred years sluggish and dissipated. [13]

113. Yo ca vassasataṃ jīve apassaṃ udayabbayaṃ,
ekāhaṃ jīvitaṃ seyyo passato udayabbayaṃ.

113. Better it is to live one day seeing the rise and fall of things than to live a hundred years without ever seeing the rise and fall of things. [14]

114. Yo ca vassasataṃ jīve apassaṃ amataṃ padaṃ,
ekāhaṃ jīvitaṃ seyyo passato amataṃ padaṃ.

114. Better it is to live one day seeing the Deathless than to live a hundred years without ever seeing the Deathless. [15]

115. Yo ca vassasataṃ jīve apassaṃ dhammam uttamaṃ,
ekāhaṃ jīvitaṃ seyyo passato dhammam uttamaṃ.

115. Better it is to live one day seeing the Supreme Truth than to live a hundred years without ever seeing the Supreme Truth. [16]

9
Pāpavagga
Evil

116. Abhittharetha kalyāṇe, pāpā cittaṃ nivāraye,
dandhaṃ hi karoto puññaṃ pāpasmiṃ ramatī mano.

116. Hasten to do good and restrain your mind from evil. When one is slow in doing good, one's mind delights in evil. [1]

117. Pāpañ ce puriso kayirā na taṃ kayirā punappunaṃ,
na tamhi chandaṃ kayirātha, dukkho pāpassa uccayo.

117. Should a person commit evil, let him not do it again and again. Let him not form a desire for it, for painful is the -accumulation of evil. [2]

118. Puññañ ce puriso kayirā kayirāth'etaṃ punappunaṃ,
tamhi chandaṃ kayirātha, sukho puññassa uccayo.

118. Should a person do good, let him do it again and again. Let him form a desire for it, for blissful is the accumulation of good. [3]

119. Pāpo pi passatī bhadraṃ yāva pāpaṃ na paccati,
yadā ca paccatī pāpaṃ atha pāpo pāpāni passati.

119. It may be well with the evil-doer as long as the evil has not ripened, but when it does ripen, then the evil-doer sees (the painful results of) his evil deeds. [4]

120. Bhadro pi passatī pāpaṃ yāva bhadraṃ na paccati,
yadā ca paccatī bhadraṃ atha bhadro bhadrāni passati.

120. It may be ill with the doer of good as long as the good has not ripened, but when it does ripen, then the doer of good sees (the pleasant results of) his good deeds. [5]

121. Māvamaññetha pāpassa "Na maṃ taṃ āgamissati,"
udabindunipātena udakumbho pi pūrati,
pūrati bālo pāpassa thokathokam pi ācinaṃ.

121. Do not think lightly of evil, saying, "It will not come to me." Drop by drop is the water pot filled; likewise the fool, gathering it little by little, fills himself with evil. [6]

122. Māvamaññetha puññassa "Na maṃ taṃ āgamissati,"
udabindunipātena udakumbho pi pūrati,
pūrati dhīro puññassa thokathokam pi ācinaṃ.

122. Do not think lightly of good, saying, "It will not come to me." Drop by drop is the water pot filled; likewise the wise man, gathering it little by little, fills himself with good. [7]

123. Vāṇijo va bhayaṃ maggaṃ appasattho mahaddhano,
visaṃ jivitukāmo va pāpāni parivajjaye.

123. Just as a trader with a small escort and great wealth would avoid a perilous route, or just as one desiring to live avoids poison, even so should one shun evil deeds. [8]

124. Pāṇimhi ce vaṇo nāssa hareyya pāṇinā visam;
nābbaṇam visam anveti natthi pāpam akubbato.

124. If on the hand there is no wound, one may even carry poison in it. Poison does not affect one who is free from wounds, and for him who does no evil, there is no ill. [9]

125. Yo appaduṭṭhassa narassa dussati suddhassa posassa anaṅgaṇassa,
tam eva bālaṃ pacceti pāpaṃ sukhumo rajo paṭivātaṃ va khitto.

125. Like fine dust thrown against the wind, evil falls back upon that fool who offends an inoffensive, pure, and guiltless man. [10]

126. Gabbham eke uppajjanti nirayaṃ pāpakammino,
saggaṃ sugatino yanti parinibbanti anāsavā.

126. Some are born in the womb; the wicked are born in hell; the devout go to heaven; the canker-free attain Nibbāna. [11]

127. Na antalikkhe na samuddamajjhe na pabbatānaṃ
vivaraṃ pavissa
na vijjatī so jagatippadeso yatthaṭṭhito muñceyya
pāpakammā.

127. Neither in the sky, nor in mid-ocean, nor by entering into mountain clefts—nowhere in the world is there a place where one may escape from the result of an evil deed. [12]

128. Na antalikkhe na samuddamajjhe na pabbatānaṃ
vivaraṃ pavissa
na vijjatī so jagatippadeso yatthaṭṭhito nappasaheyya
maccu.

128. Neither in the sky, nor in mid-ocean, nor by entering into mountain clefts—nowhere in the world is there a place where one will not be overcome by death. [13]

10

Daṇḍavagga
Violence

129. Sabbe tasanti daṇḍassa sabbe bhāyanti maccuno,
attānaṃ upamaṃ katvā na haneyya na ghātaye.

129. All tremble at violence, all fear death. Putting oneself in the place of another, one should not kill nor cause another to kill. [1]

130. Sabbe tasanti daṇḍassa sabbesaṃ jīvitaṃ piyaṃ,
attānaṃ upamaṃ katvā na haneyya na ghātaye.

130. All tremble at violence, life is dear to all. Putting oneself in the place of another, one should not kill nor cause another to kill. [2]

131. Sukhakāmāni bhūtāni yo daṇḍena vihiṃsati,
attano sukham esāno pecca so na labhate sukhaṃ.

131. One who, while himself seeking happiness, oppresses with violence other beings who also desire happiness, will not attain happiness hereafter. [3]

132. Sukhakāmāni bhūtāni yo daṇḍena na hiṃsati,
attano sukham esāno pecca so labhate sukhaṃ.

132. One who, while himself seeking happiness, does not oppress with violence other beings who also desire happiness, will find happiness hereafter. [4]

133. Māvoca pharusaṃ kañci, vuttā paṭivadeyyu taṃ,
dukkhā hi sārambhakathā paṭidaṇḍā phuseyyu taṃ.

133. Do not speak harshly to anyone; for those thus spoken to might retort. Indeed, vindictive speech hurts, and retaliation may overtake you. [5]

134. Sace neresi attānaṃ kaṃso upahato yathā,
esa patto'si nibbānaṃ, sārambho te na vijjati.

134. If, like a broken gong, you silence yourself, you have approached Nibbāna, for vindictiveness is no more in you. [6]

135. Yathā daṇḍena gopālo gāvo pājeti gocaraṃ,
evaṃ jarā ca maccū ca āyuṃ pājenti pāṇinaṃ.

135. Just as a cowherd drives the cattle to pasture with a staff, so do old age and death drive the life force of beings (from existence to existence). [7]

136. Atha pāpāni kammāni karaṃ bālo na bujjhati,
sehi kammehi dummedho aggidaḍḍho va tappati.

136. When the fool commits evil deeds, he does not realize (their evil nature). The witless man is tormented by his own deeds like one burnt by fire. [8]

137. Yo daṇḍena adaṇḍesu appaduṭṭhesu dussati,
dasannam aññataraṃ ṭhānaṃ khippam eva nigacchati.

137. One who uses violence against those who are unarmed, and offends those who are inoffensive, will soon come upon one of these ten states: [9]

138. Vedanaṃ pharusaṃ jāniṃ, sarīrassa ca bhedanaṃ,
garukaṃ vāpi ābādhaṃ, cittakkhepaṃ va pāpuṇe.

138. He will incur sharp pain, disaster, and bodily injury, or serious illness, or derangement of mind. [10]

139. Rājato va upasaggaṃ, abbhakkhānaṃ va dāruṇaṃ,
parikkhayaṃ va ñātīnaṃ, bhogānaṃ va pabhaṅguraṃ.

139. Or he will meet wth trouble from the government, or grave charges, loss of relatives, or loss of wealth. [11]

140. Atha vā'ssa agārāni aggi ḍahati pāvako,
kāyassa bhedā duppañño nirayaṃ sopapajjati.

140. Or his houses will be destroyed by a ravaging fire, and upon dissolution of the body that ignorant person will be reborn in hell. [12]

141. Na naggacariyā na jaṭā na paṅkā nānāsakā thaṇḍilasāyikā vā,
rajo ca jallaṃ ukkuṭikappadhānaṃ sodhenti maccaṃ avitiṇṇakaṅkhaṃ.

141. Neither going about naked, nor matted locks, nor filth, nor fasting, nor lying on the ground, nor smearing oneself with ashes and dust, nor sitting on the heels (in penance) can purify a mortal who has not overcome mental wavering. [13]

142. Alaṅkato ce pi samañ careyya santo danto niyato brahmacārī
sabbesu bhūtesu nidhāya daṇḍaṃ so brāhmaṇo so samaṇo sa bhikkhu.

142. Even though he be well adorned, yet if he is poised, calm, controlled, and established in the holy life, having laid aside violence towards all beings—he, truly, is a holy man, a renunciate, a monk. [14]

143. Hirīnisedho puriso koci lokasmiṃ vijjati
yo nindaṃ apabodheti, asso bhadro kasām iva.

143. Only rarely is there a man in this world who, restrained by modesty, avoids reproach, as a thoroughbred horse avoids the whip. [15]

144. Asso yathā bhadro kasāniviṭṭho ātāpino saṃvegino bhavātha;
saddhāya sīlena ca viriyena ca samādhinā dhammavinicchayena ca
sampannavijjācaraṇā patissatā pahassatha dukkham idaṃ anappakaṃ.

144. Like a thoroughbred horse touched by the whip, be strenuous, be filled with spiritual yearning. By faith and moral

purity, by effort and meditation, by investigation of the truth, by being rich in knowledge and virtue, and by being mindful, destroy this unlimited suffering. [16]

> *145. Udakaṃ hi nayanti nettikā, usukārā namayanti tejanaṃ,*
> *dāruṃ namayanti tacchakā, attānaṃ damayanti subbatā.*

145. Irrigators regulate the waters; arrow-makers straighten arrow shafts; carpenters shape wood; and the good control themselves. [17]

11

Jarāvagga
Old Age

146. Ko nu hāso kim ānando niccaṃ pajjalite sati?
Andhakārena onaddhā padīpaṃ na gavessatha?

146. When this world is ever ablaze, why this laughter, why this jubilation? Shrouded in darkness, why don't you seek the light? [1]

147. Passa cittakataṃ bimbaṃ arukāyaṃ samussitaṃ
āturaṃ bahusaṅkappaṃ yassa natthi dhuvaṃ ṭhiti.

147. Behold this body, a painted image, a mass of heaped up sores—infirm, full of hankering, with nothing lasting or stable. [2]

148. Parijiṇṇaṃ idaṃ rūpaṃ roganiḍḍhaṃ pabhaṅguraṃ,
bhijjati pūtisandeho maraṇantaṃ hi jīvitaṃ.

148. Fully worn out is this body, a nest of disease, and fragile. This foul mass breaks up, for life ends in death. [3]

149. Yān'imāni apatthāni alāpūn'eva sārade
kāpotakāni aṭṭhīni tāni disvāna kā rati?

149. These dove-coloured bones are like gourds that lie scattered about in autumn; having seen them, how can one seek delight? [4]

150. Aṭṭhīnaṃ nagaraṃ kataṃ maṃsalohitalepanaṃ
yattha jarā ca maccū ca māno makkho ca ohito.

150. The body is a city built of bones, plastered with flesh and blood, containing within decay and death, pride and contempt. [5]

151. Jīranti ve rājarathā sucittā atho sarīram pi jaraṃ upeti, satañ ca dhammo na jaraṃ upeti, santo have sabbhi pavedayanti.

151. Even gorgeous royal chariots wear out, and this body too wears out. But the Dhamma of the good does not age; thus the good make it known to the good. [6]

152. Appassut'āyaṃ puriso balivaddo va jīrati;
maṃsāni tassa vaḍḍhanti, paññā tassa na vaḍḍhati.

152. The man of little learning grows old like a bull: he grows only in bulk, but his wisdom does not grow. [7]

153. Anekajātisaṃsāraṃ sandhāvissaṃ anibbisaṃ
gahakārakaṃ gavesanto: dukkhā jāti punappunaṃ.

153. Through many a birth in saṃsāra have I wandered in vain, seeking the builder of this house (of life). Repeated birth is indeed suffering! [8]

154. Gahakāraka diṭṭho'si puna gehaṃ na kāhasi,
sabbā te phāsukā bhaggā, gahakūṭaṃ visaṅkhitaṃ;
visaṅkhāragataṃ cittaṃ taṇhānaṃ khayam ajjhagā.

154. O house-builder, you are seen! You will not build this house again. For all your rafters are broken and your ridgepole shattered. My mind has reached the Unconditioned: I have attained the destruction of cravings.[13] [9]

155. Acaritvā brahmacariyaṃ aladdhā yobbane dhanaṃ,
jiṇṇakoñcā va jhāyanti khīṇamacche va pallale.

155. Those who in youth have not led the holy life, who have failed to acquire wealth, languish like old cranes in a pond without fish. [10]

---

13. According to the commentary, vv. 153–154 are the Buddha's "Song of Victory," his first utterance after his Enlightenment. The house is individualized existence in saṃsara; the house-builder craving; the rafters the passions; and the ridge-pole ignorance.

156. Acaritvā brahmacariyaṃ, aladdhā yobbane dhanaṃ,
senti cāpātikhīṇā va purāṇāni anutthunaṃ.

156. Those who in youth have not led the holy life, who have failed to acquire wealth, lie like worn-out arrows (shot from) a bow, sighing over the past. [11]

12

Attavagga

The Self

> *157. Attānañ ce piyaṃ jaññā, rakkheyya naṃ surakkhitaṃ;*
> *tiṇṇaṃ aññataraṃ yāmaṃ paṭijaggeyya paṇḍito.*

157. If one holds oneself dear, one should diligently watch oneself. Let the wise person keep vigil during any of the three watches of the night. [1]

> *158. Attānam eva paṭhamaṃ patirūpe nivesaye,*
> *ath'aññam anusāseyya, na kilisseyya paṇḍito.*

158. One should first establish oneself in what is proper; then only should one instruct others. Thus the wise person will not be reproached. [2]

> *159. Attānañ ce tathā kayirā yath'aññam anusāsati,*
> *sudanto vata dammetha attā hi kira duddamo.*

159. One should do what one teaches others to do; if one would train others, one should be well-controlled oneself. Difficult, indeed, is self-control. [3]

> *160. Attā hi attano nātho; ko hi nātho paro siyā?*
> *Attanā va suddantena nāthaṃ labhati dullabhaṃ.*

160. One is truly one's protector. Who else could the protector be? With oneself fully controlled one gains a protector which is hard to gain. [4]

> *161. Attanā va kataṃ pāpaṃ attajaṃ attasambhavaṃ,*
> *abhimanthati dummedhaṃ vajiraṃ v'asmamayaṃ maṇiṃ.*

161. The evil a witless person does by himself, born of himself and produced by himself, grinds him as a diamond grinds a hard gem. [5]

162. Yassa accantadussīlyaṃ māluvā sālam iv'otthataṃ
karoti so tath'attānaṃ yathā naṃ icchatī diso.

162. Just as a jungle creeper strangles the tree on which it grows, even so a person who is exceedingly depraved harms himself as an enemy might wish. [6]

163. Sukarāni asādhūni attano ahitāni ca,
yaṃ ve hitañ ca sādhuñ ca, taṃ ve paramadukkaraṃ.

163. Easy to do are things that are bad and harmful to oneself, but exceedingly difficult to do are things that are good and beneficial. [7]

164. Yo sāsanaṃ arahataṃ ariyānaṃ dhammajīvinaṃ,
paṭikkosati dummedho diṭṭhiṃ nissāya pāpikaṃ,
phalāni kaṭṭhakasseva attaghaññāya phallati.

164. Whoever, on account of perverted views, reviles the teaching of the arahats, the noble ones of righteous life—that fool, like the bamboo, produces fruits only for self-destruction.[14] [8]

165. Attanā va kataṃ pāpaṃ attanā saṅkilissati;
attanā akataṃ pāpaṃ attanā va visujjhati;
suddhi asuddhi paccattaṃ nāñño aññaṃ visodhaye.

165. By oneself is evil done, by oneself is one defiled. By oneself is evil left undone, by oneself is one purified. Purity and impurity depend on oneself—no one can purify another. [9]

166. Attadatthaṃ paratthena bahunā pi na hāpaye;
attadatthaṃ abhiññāya sadatthapasuto siyā.

166. Let one not neglect one's own welfare for the sake of another, however great. Clearly understanding one's own welfare, let one be intent upon the good. [10]

14. Certain reeds of the bamboo family perish immediately after producing fruits.

13
Lokavagga
The World

167. Hīnaṃ dhammaṃ na seveyya, pamādena na saṃvase;
micchādiṭṭhiṃ na seveyya, na siyā lokavaḍḍhano.

167. Do not follow the vulgar way; do not live in heedlessness; do not hold false views; do not linger long in worldly existence. [1]

168. Uttiṭṭhe nappamajjeyya, dhammaṃ sucaritañ care,
dhammacārī sukhaṃ seti asmiṃ loke paramhi ca.

168. Arise! Do not be heedless! Lead a life of good conduct. The righteous live happily both in this world and the next. [2]

169. Dhammañ care sucaritaṃ, na naṃ duccaritañ care,
dhammacārī sukhaṃ seti asmiṃ loke paramhi ca.

169. Lead a life of good conduct. Do not lead a base life. The righteous live happily both in this world and the next. [3]

170. Yathā bubbulakaṃ passe, yathā passe marīcikaṃ,
evaṃ lokaṃ avekkhantaṃ maccurājā na passati.

170. When one looks upon the world as a bubble and a mirage, the King of Death does not see one. [4]

171. Etha passath'imaṃ lokaṃ, cittaṃ rājarathūpamaṃ,
yattha bālā visīdanti natthi saṅgo vijānataṃ.

171. Come! Behold this world, which is like a decorated royal chariot. Here fools flounder, but the wise have no attachment to it. [5]

172. Yo ca pubbe pamajjitvā pacchā so nappamajjati;
so imaṃ lokaṃ pabhāseti, abbhā mutto va candimā.

172. One who having been heedless is heedless no more, illuminates this world like the moon freed from a cloud. [6]

173. Yassa pāpaṃ kataṃ kammaṃ kusalena pithīyati,
so imaṃ lokaṃ pabhāseti, abbhā mutto va candimā.

173. One who by good covers the evil he has done, illuminates this world like the moon freed from a cloud. [7]

174. Andhabhūto ayaṃ loko tanuk'ettha vipassati,
sakunto jālamutto va appo saggāya gacchati.

174. Blind is this world; here only a few possess insight. Only a few, like birds escaping from a net, go to the realm of bliss. [8]

175. Haṃsādiccapathe yanti, ākāse yanti iddhiyā;
nīyanti dhīrā lokamhā jetvā māraṃ savāhiniṃ.

175. Swans fly on the path of the sun; men pass through the air by psychic powers; the wise are led away from the world after vanquishing Māra and his host. [9]

176. Ekaṃ dhammaṃ atītassa musāvādissa jantuno
vitiṇṇaparalokassa natthi pāpaṃ akāriyaṃ.

176. For a liar who has violated the one law (of truthfulness), who holds in scorn the hereafter, there is no evil that he cannot do. [10]

177. Na ve kadariyā devalokaṃ vajanti, bālā have nappasaṃsanti dānaṃ,
dhīro ca dānaṃ anumodamāno ten'eva so hoti sukhī parattha.

177. Truly, misers fare not to heavenly realms; nor, indeed, do fools praise generosity. But the wise person rejoices in giving, and by that alone does he become happy here-after. [11]

178. Pathavyā ekarajjena, saggassa gamanena vā,
sabbalokādhipaccena, sotāpattiphalaṃ varaṃ.

178. Better than sole sovereignty over the earth, better than going to heaven, better even than lordship over all the worlds is the fruition of stream-entry.[15] [12]

15. Stream-entry (*sotāpatti*): the first stage of supramundane attainment.

14

Buddhavaga
The Buddha

> *179. Yassa jitaṃ nāvajīyati, jitam assa no yāti koci loke,*
> *taṃ Buddham anantagocaraṃ apadaṃ kena padena nessatha?*

179. By what track can you trace that trackless one, the Buddha of limitless range, whose victory nothing can undo, whom none of the vanquished defilements can ever pursue? [1]

> *180. Yassa jālinī visattikā taṇhā natthi kuhiñci netave,*
> *taṃ Buddham anantagocaraṃ apadaṃ kena padena nessatha?*

180. By what track can you trace that trackless one, the Buddha of limitless range, in whom exists no longer the entangling and embroiling craving that perpetuates becoming? [2]

> *181. Ye jhānapasutā dhīrā nekkhammūpasame ratā,*
> *devāpi tesaṃ pihayanti sambuddhānaṃ satīmataṃ.*

181. Those wise ones who are devoted to meditation and who delight in the calm of renunciation—such mindful ones, Supreme Buddhas, even the gods hold dear. [3]

> *182. Kiccho manussapaṭilābho, kicchaṃ maccāna jīvitaṃ,*
> *kicchaṃ saddhammasavaṇaṃ, kiccho Buddhānaṃ uppādo.*

182. Hard is it to be born a human being, hard is the life of mortals. Hard is it to gain the opportunity to hear the Good Dhamma, and hard, indeed, to encounter the arising of the Buddhas. [4]

> *183. Sabbapāpassa akaraṇaṃ, kusalassa upasampadā,*
> *sacittapariyodapanaṃ, etaṃ Buddhāna sāsanaṃ.*

183. To avoid all evil, to cultivate good, and to cleanse one's own mind—this is the teaching of the Buddhas. [5]

184. Khantī paramaṃ tapo titikkhā, nibbānaṃ paramaṃ vadanti Buddhā;
na hi pabbajito parūpaghātī, samaṇo hoti paraṃ viheṭhayanto.

184. Enduring patience is the highest austerity. "Nibbāna is supreme," say the Buddhas. He is not a true monk who harms another, nor a real renunciate who oppresses others. [6]

185. Anūpavādo anūpaghāto, pātimokkhe ca saṃvaro
mattaññutā ca bhattasmiṃ, pantañ ca sayanāsanaṃ,
adhicitte ca āyogo, etaṃ Buddhāna sāsanaṃ.

185. Not despising, not harming, restraint according to the code of monastic discipline, moderation in food, dwelling in solitude, devotion to meditation—this is the teaching of the Buddhas. [7]

186. Na kahāpaṇavassena titti kāmesu vijjati,
appassādā dukhā kāmā iti viññāya paṇḍito.

187. Api dibbesu kāmesu ratiṃ so nādhigacchati,
taṇhakkhayarato hoti sammāsambuddhasāvako.

186–187. There is no satisfying sensual desires even with a rain of gold coins, for sense pleasures give little satisfaction and entail much pain. Having understood this, the wise man finds no delight even in heavenly pleasures. The disciple of the Supreme Buddha delights in the destruction of craving. [8-9]

188. Bahuṃ ve saraṇaṃ yanti, pabbatāni vanāni ca
ārāma-rukkha-cetyāni, manussā bhayatajjitā.

188. People, driven by fear, go for refuge to many places—to hills, woods, groves, trees, and shrines. [10]

189. N'etaṃ kho saraṇaṃ khemaṃ n'etaṃ saraṇam uttamaṃ,
n'etaṃ saraṇam āgamma sabbadukkhā pamuccati.

189. This, indeed, is no safe refuge; this is not the refuge supreme. Not by resorting to such a refuge is one released from all suffering. [11]

190. Yo ca Buddhañ ca dhammañ ca saṅghañ ca saraṇaṃ gato,
cattāri ariyasaccāni, sammappaññāya passati.

191. Dukkhaṃ dukkhasamuppādaṃ, dukkhassa ca atikkamaṃ,
ariyañ c'aṭṭhaṅgikaṃ maggaṃ, dukkhūpasamagāminaṃ.

190–191. One who has gone for refuge to the Buddha, the Dhamma, and the Sangha, penetrates with wisdom the Four Noble Truths—suffering, the cause of suffering, the cessation of suffering, and the Noble Eightfold Path leading to the cessation of suffering.[16] [12-13]

192. Etaṃ kho saraṇaṃ khemaṃ etaṃ saraṇam uttamaṃ,
etaṃ saraṇam āgamma sabbadukkhā pamuccati.

192. This, indeed, is the safe refuge, this is the refuge supreme. Having gone to such a refuge, one is released from all suffering. [14]

193. Dullabho purisājañño, na so sabbattha jāyati,
yattha so jāyati dhīro taṃ kulaṃ sukham edhati.

193. Hard to find is the thoroughbred man (the Buddha). He is not born everywhere. Where such a wise man is born, that clan thrives happily. [15]

---

16. The Sangha: both the monastic order (*bhikkhu-saṅgha*) and the order of noble ones (*ariya-saṅgha*) who have reached the four supramundane stages.

194. Sukho Buddhānaṃ uppādo, sukhā saddhammadesanā,
sukhā saṅghassa sāmaggi, samaggānaṃ tapo sukho.

194. Blessed is the birth of the Buddhas; blessed is the enunciation of the Good Dhamma; blessed is harmony in the Sangha; and blessed is the spiritual pursuit of the united truth-seekers. [16]

195. Pūjārahe pūjayato Buddhe yadi va sāvake
papañca-samatikkante tiṇṇa-soka-pariddave

196. Te tādise pūjayato, nibbute akutobhaye,
na sakkā puññaṃ saṅkhātuṃ, im'ettam iti kena ci.

195–196. One who reveres those worthy of reverence, the Buddhas and their disciples, who have transcended all worldliness and passed beyond the reach of sorrow and lamentation—one who reveres such peaceful and fearless ones, his merit none can compute by any measure. [17-18]

15
Sukhavagga
Happiness

197. Susukhaṃ vata jīvāma verinesu averino;
verinesu manussesu viharāma averino.

197. Happy indeed we live, friendly amidst the hostile! Amidst hostile people we dwell free from hatred. [1]

198. Susukhaṃ vata jīvāma āturesu anāturā;
āturesu manussesu viharāma anāturā.

198. Happy indeed we live, unafflicted amidst those afflicted (by craving)! Amidst afflicted people we dwell free from affliction. [2]

199. Susukhaṃ vata jīvāma ussukesu anussukā;
ussukesu manussesu viharāma anussukā.

199. Happy indeed we live, free from avarice amidst the avaricious! Amidst avaricious people we dwell free from avarice. [3]

200. Susukhaṃ vata jīvāma yesaṃ no natthi kiñcanaṃ;
pītibhakkhā bhavissāma devā ābhassarā yathā.

200. Happy indeed we live, we who possess nothing! We shall be feeders on joy, like the radiant gods.[17] [4]

201. Jayaṃ veraṃ pasavati, dukkhaṃ seti parājito;
upasanto sukhaṃ seti hitvā jayaparājayaṃ.

201. Victory begets enmity, the defeated dwell in pain. Happily the peaceful live, discarding both victory and defeat. [5]

202. Natthi rāgasamo aggi, natthi dosasamo kali,
natthi khandhasamā dukkhā, natthi santiparaṃ sukhaṃ.

---

17. The radiant gods (*devā ābhassarā*): a class of gods in the realm of subtle form (*rūpa-dhātu*); they are said to subsist on joy instead of food.

202. There is no fire like lust, no crime like hatred. There is no ill like the aggregates, no bliss higher than the peace (of Nibbāna).[18] [6]

> *203. Jighacchāparamā rogā, saṅkhārā paramā dukhā,*
> *etaṃ ñatvā yathābhūtaṃ nibbānaṃ paramaṃ sukhaṃ.*

203. Hunger is the worst disease, conditioned things the worst suffering. Knowing this as it really is, the wise realize Nibbāna, the highest bliss. [7]

> *204. Ārogyaparamā lābhā, santuṭṭhiparamaṃ dhanaṃ,*
> *vissāsaparamā ñātī, nibbānaṃ paramaṃ sukhaṃ.*

204. Health is the highest gain, contentment the greatest wealth. A trustworthy person is the best kinsman, Nibbāna the highest bliss. [8]

> *205. Pavivekarasaṃ pītvā rasaṃ upasamassa ca*
> *niddaro hoti nippāpo dhammapītirasaṃ pibaṃ.*

205. Having savoured the taste of solitude and of peace, pain-free and stainless he becomes, drinking deep the taste of the bliss of the Dhamma. [9]

> *206. Sāhu dassanam ariyānaṃ sannivāso sadā sukho,*
> *adassanena bālānaṃ niccam eva sukhī siyā.*

206. Good it is to see the noble ones, to live with them is ever blissful. One will always be happy by not encountering fools. [10]

> *207. Bālasaṅgatacārī hi dīgham addhāna socati,*
> *dukkho bālehi saṃvāso amitten'eva sabbadā,*
> *dhīro ca sukhasaṃvāso ñātīnaṃ va samāgamo.*

207. Indeed, one who moves in the company of fools grieves for a long time. Association with fools is ever painful, like

---

18. Aggregates (*khandha*): the five groups into which the Buddha analyzes the living being—material form, feeling, perception, mental formations, and consciousness.

partnership with an enemy. But happy is association with the wise, like meeting one's own relatives. [11]

> 208. *Tasmā hi: dhīrañ ca paññañ ca bahussutañ ca*
> *dhorayhasīlaṃ vatavantam āriyaṃ,*
> *taṃ tādisaṃ sappurisaṃ sumedhaṃ bhajetha*
> *nakkhattapathaṃ va candimā.*

208. Therefore, follow the noble one, who is steadfast, wise, learned, dutiful, and devout. One should follow only such a person, who is truly good and discerning, even as the moon follows the path of the stars. [12]

16

Piyavagga

Affection

209. Ayoge yuñjam attānaṃ yogasmiñ ca ayojayaṃ,
atthaṃ hitvā piyaggāhī pihet'attānuyoginaṃ.

209. Giving himself to things to be shunned and not exerting himself where exertion is needed, a seeker after pleasures forsakes his own true welfare and will come to envy those intent upon their welfare. [1]

210. Mā piyehi samāgañchi, appiyehi kudācanaṃ,
piyānaṃ adassanaṃ dukkhaṃ appiyānañ ca dassanaṃ.

210. Seek no intimacy with the beloved and also not with the unloved, for not to see the beloved and to see the unloved are both painful. [2]

211. Tasmā piyaṃ na kayirātha, piyāpāyo hi pāpako,
ganthā tesaṃ na vijjanti yesaṃ natthi piyāppiyaṃ.

211. Therefore, hold nothing dear, for separation from the dear is painful. There are no bonds for those who have nothing beloved or unloved. [3]

212. Piyato jāyatī soko, piyato jāyatī bhayaṃ,
piyato vippamuttassa . natthi soko kuto bhayaṃ?

212. From endearment springs grief, from endearment springs fear. For one who is wholly free from endearment there is no grief, whence then fear? [4]

213. Pemato jāyatī soko, Pemato jāyatī bhayaṃ,
Pemato vippamuttassa natthi soko kuto bhayaṃ?

213. From affection springs grief, from affection springs fear. For one who is wholly free from affection there is no grief, whence then fear? [5]

214. Ratiyā jāyatī soko, ratiyā jāyatī bhayaṃ,
ratiyā vippamuttassa natthi soko kuto bhayaṃ?

214. From enjoyment springs grief, from enjoyment springs fear. For one who is wholly free from enjoyment there is no grief, whence then fear? [6]

215. Kāmato jāyatī soko, kāmato jāyatī bhayaṃ,
kāmato vippamuttassa natthi soko kuto bhayaṃ?

215. From lust springs grief, from lust springs fear. For one who is wholly free from lust there is no grief, whence then fear? [7]

216. Taṇhāya jāyatī soko, taṇhāya jāyatī bhayaṃ,
taṇhāya vippamuttassa natthi soko kuto bhayaṃ?

216. From craving springs grief, from craving springs fear. For one who is wholly free from craving there is no grief, whence then fear? [8]

217. Sīladassanasampannaṃ dhammaṭṭhaṃ saccavedinaṃ
attano kammakubbānaṃ taṃ jano kurute piyaṃ.

217. People hold dear one who embodies virtue and insight, who is principled, has realized the truth, and who himself does what he ought to be doing. [9]

218. Chandajāto anakkhāte, manasā ca phuṭo siyā,
kāmesu ca appaṭibaddhacitto, uddhaṃsoto ti vuccati.

218. One who is intent upon the Ineffable (Nibbāna) and dwells with mind inspired (by wisdom), such a person—no more bound by sense pleasures—is called "one bound upstream."[19] [10]

219. Cirappavāsiṃ purisaṃ dūrato sotthim āgataṃ,
ñātimittā suhajjā ca, abhinandanti āgataṃ.

19. One bound upstream: a particular type of non-returner (*anāgāmi*).

219. When, after a long absence, a man safely returns home from afar, his relatives, friends, and well-wishers welcome him home on arrival. [11]

> 220. *Tath'eva katapuññam pi asmā lokā paraṃ gataṃ,*
> *puññāni paṭigaṇhanti piyaṃ ñātiṃ va āgataṃ.*

220. As relatives welcome a dear one on arrival, even so his own good deeds will welcome the doer of good who has gone from this world to the next. [12]

17

Kodhavagga

Anger

221. Kodhaṃ jahe vippajaheyya mānaṃ, saññojanaṃ sabbam atikkameyya;
taṃ nāmarūpasmiṃ asajjamānaṃ akiñcanaṃ nānupatanti dukkhā.

221. One should give up anger, renounce pride, and overcome all fetters. Suffering never befalls him who clings not to mind and body and is detached. [1]

222. Yo ve uppatitaṃ kodhaṃ rathaṃ bhantaṃ va dhāraye,
tam ahaṃ sārathiṃ brūmi, rasmiggāho itaro jano.

222. One who checks rising anger as a charioteer checks a rolling chariot, him I call a true charioteer; others only hold the reins. [2]

223. Akkodhena jine kodhaṃ, asādhuṃ sādhunā jine,
jine kadariyaṃ dānena, saccena alikavādinaṃ.

223. Overcome the angry by non-anger; overcome the wicked by goodness; overcome the miser by generosity; overcome the liar by truth. [3]

224. Saccaṃ bhaṇe na kujjheyya, dajjā appasmim pi yācito,
etehi tīhi ṭhānehi gacche devāna santike.

224. Speak the truth; do not give way to anger; give of your little to him that asks of you; by these three things one may go to the realm of gods. [4]

225. Ahiṃsakā ye munayo, niccaṃ kāyena saṃvutā,
te yanti accutaṃ ṭhānaṃ, yattha gantvā na socare.

225. Those sages who are inoffensive and ever restrained in body, go to the deathless state, where they grieve no more. [5]

226. Sadā jāgaramānānaṃ, ahorattānusikkhinaṃ,
nibbānaṃ adhimuttānaṃ, atthaṃ gacchanti āsavā.

226. Those who are ever vigilant, who discipline themselves day and night, ever intent upon Nibbāna—their cankers fade away. [6]

227. Porāṇam etaṃ Atula n'etaṃ ajjatanām iva,
nindanti tuṇhim āsīnaṃ, nindanti bahubhāṇinaṃ,
mitabhāṇinam pi nindanti, natthi loke anindito.

227. O Atula! Indeed, this is an old pattern, not one only of today: they blame one who remains silent, they blame one who speaks much, they blame one who speaks in moderation. There is none in this world who is not blamed. [7]

228. Na c'āhu na ca bhavissati, na c'etarahi vijjati,
ekantaṃ nindito poso, ekantaṃ vā pasaṃsito.

228. There never was, there never will be, nor is there now, a person who is wholly blamed or wholly praised. [8]

229. Yañ ce viññū pasaṃsanti anuvicca suve suve
acchiddavuttiṃ medhāviṃ paññāsīlasamāhitaṃ—
230. Nekkhaṃ jambonadasseva ko taṃ ninditum arahati?
devā pi taṃ pasaṃsanti, Brahmunā pi pasaṃsito.

229–230. But as to the person whom the wise praise after observing him day after day, one of flawless character, wise, and endowed with knowledge and virtue—who can blame such a one, as worthy as a coin of refined gold? Even the gods praise him; by Brahmā, too, is he praised. [9-10]

231. Kāyappakopaṃ rakkheyya, kāyena saṃvuto siyā,
kāyaduccaritaṃ hitvā kāyena sucaritaṃ care.

231. One should guard oneself against irritability in bodily action; one should be controlled in deed. Having abandoned bodily misconduct, one should practise good conduct in deed. [11]

232. Vacīpakopaṃ rakkheyya, vācāya saṃvuto siyā,
vacīduccaritaṃ hitvā vācāya sucaritaṃ care.

232. One should guard oneself against irritability in speech; one should be controlled in speech. Having abandoned verbal misconduct, one should practise good conduct in speech. [12]

233. Manopakopaṃ rakkheyya, manasā saṃvuto siyā,
manoduccaritaṃ hitvā manasā sucaritaṃ care.

233. One should guard oneself against irritability in thought; one should be controlled in thought. Having abandoned mental misconduct, one should practise good conduct in thought. [13]

234. Kāyena saṃvutā dhīrā atho vācāya saṃvutā
manasā saṃvutā dhīrā te ve suparisaṃvutā.

234. The wise are controlled in bodily deeds, controlled in speech, and controlled in thought. They are truly well controlled. [14]

18
Malavagga
Impurity

235. Paṇḍupalāso va dāni'si, yamapurisā pi ca tam upaṭṭhitā,
uyyogamukhe ca tiṭṭhasi, pātheyyam pi ca te na vijjati.

235. Like a withered leaf are you now; death's messengers are waiting for you. You stand on the eve of your departure, yet you have made no provision for your journey! [1]

236. So karohi dīpam attano, khippaṃ vāyama paṇḍito bhava;
niddhantamalo anaṅgaṇo dibbaṃ ariyabhūmim ehisi.

236. Make an island for yourself! Strive hard and become wise! Rid of impurities and cleansed of stain, you shall enter the celestial abode of the noble ones. [2]

237. Upanītavayo va dāni'si, sampayāto'si Yamassa santike,
vāso pi ca te natthi antarā, pātheyyam pi ca te na vijjati.

237. Your life has come to an end now; you are setting forth into the presence of Yama, the King of Death. No resting place is there for you on the way, yet you have made no provision for your journey! [3]

238. So karohi dīpam attano, khippaṃ vāyama paṇḍito bhava;
niddhantamalo anaṅgaṇo na puna jātijaraṃ upehisi.

238. Make an island for yourself! Strive hard and become wise! Rid of impurities and cleansed of stain, you shall not come again to birth and decay. [4]

239. Anupubbena medhāvī thokathokaṃ khaṇe khaṇe
kammāro rajatasseva niddhame malam attano.

239. One by one, little by little, moment by moment, a wise man should remove his own impurities, as a smith removes the dross of silver. [5]

240. Ayasā va malaṃ samuṭṭhitaṃ, taduṭṭhāya tam eva khādati,
evaṃ atidhonacārinaṃ sakakammāni nayanti duggatiṃ.

240. Just as rust arising from iron eats away the base from which it has arisen, even so their own deeds lead transgressors to a state of woe. [6]

241. Asajjhāyamalā mantā, anuṭṭhānamalā gharā,
malaṃ vaṇṇassa kosajjaṃ, pamādo rakkhato malaṃ.

241. Non-repetition is the bane of scriptures; neglect is the bane of a home; slovenliness is the bane of personal appearance; heedlessness is the bane of a watchman. [7]

242. Malitthiyā duccaritaṃ, maccheraṃ dadato malaṃ
malā ve pāpakā dhammā asmiṃ loke paramhi ca.

242. Unchastity is the taint in a woman; niggardliness is the taint in a giver. Taints, indeed, are evil things, both in this world and the next. [8]

243. Tato malā malataraṃ avijjā paramaṃ malaṃ,
etaṃ malaṃ pahatvāna nimmalā hotha bhikkhavo.

243. A worse taint than these is ignorance, the worst of all taints. Destroy this one taint and become taintless, O monks! [9]

244. Sujīvaṃ ahirikena kākasūrena dhaṃsinā
pakkhandinā pagabbhena saṅkiliṭṭhena jīvitaṃ.

244. Easy is life for the shameless one who is as impudent as a crow, back-biting and forward, arrogant and corrupt. [10]

245. Hirīmatā ca dujjīvaṃ niccaṃ sucigavesinā
alīnen'appagabbhena suddhājīvena passatā.

245. Difficult is life for the modest one who always seeks purity, who is detached and unassuming, clean in life, and discerning. [11]

246. Yo pāṇam atipāteti, musāvādañ ca bhāsati,
loke adinnaṃ ādiyati, paradārañ ca gacchati.

247. Surāmerayapānañ ca yo naro anuyuñjati,
idh'eva-m-eso lokasmiṃ mūlaṃ khaṇati attano.

246–247. One who destroys life, utters lies, takes what is not given, goes to another man's wife, and is addicted to intoxicating drinks—such a man digs up his own root even in this very world. [12-13]

248. Evaṃ bho purisa jānāhi: pāpadhammā asaññatā;
mā taṃ lobho adhammo ca ciraṃ dukkhāya randhayuṃ.

248. Know this, good man: those of evil character are uncontrolled. Let not greed and wickedness drag you to protracted misery. [14]

249. Dadāti ve yathāsaddhaṃ yathāpasādanaṃ jano,
tattha yo maṅku bhavati paresaṃ pānabhojane,
na so divā vā rattiṃ vā samādhiṃ adhigacchati.

249. People give according to their faith, according to their trust. If one becomes discontented with the food and drink given by others, one does not attain meditative absorption, either by day or by night. [15]

250. Yassa c'etaṃ samucchinnaṃ mūlaghaccaṃ samūhataṃ,
sa ve divā vā rattiṃ vā samādhiṃ adhigacchati.

250. But he in whom this (discontent) is fully destroyed, uprooted and extinct, he attains absorption, whether by day or by night. [16]

251. Natthi rāgasamo aggi, natthi dosasamo gaho,
natthi mohasamaṃ jālaṃ, natthi taṇhāsamā nadī.

251. There is no fire like lust; there is no grip like hatred; there is no net like delusion; there is no river like craving. [17]

252. Sudassaṃ vajjaṃ aññesaṃ, attano pana duddasaṃ,
paresaṃ hi so vajjāni, opuṇāti yathābhusaṃ;
attano pana chādeti, kaliṃ va kitavā saṭho.

252. Easily seen are the faults of others, but one's own are difficult to see. Like chaff one winnows another's faults but hides one's own, even as a crafty fowler hides behind sham branches. [18]

253. Paravajjānupassissa, niccaṃ ujjhānasaññino,
āsavā tassa vaḍḍhanti, ārā so āsavakkhayā.

253. He who seeks another's faults, who is ever censorious—his cankers grow. He is far from the destruction of the cankers. [19]

254. Ākāse padaṃ natthi, samaṇo natthi bāhire,
papañcābhiratā pajā, nippapañcā Tathāgatā.

254. There is no track in the sky, and no recluse outside (the Buddha's Dispensation). Humankind delights in worldliness, but the Buddhas are free from worldliness.[20] [20]

255. Ākāse padaṃ natthi, samaṇo natthi bāhire,
saṅkhārā sassatā natthi, natthi Buddhānam iñjitaṃ.

255. There is no track in the sky, and no recluse outside (the Buddha's Dispensation). There are no conditioned things that are eternal, and no instability in the Buddhas. [21]

20. Recluse (*samaṇa*): in vv.254-255 used in the special sense of those who have reached the four supramundane stages.

19

Dhammaṭṭhavagga

The Just

256. Na tena hoti dhammaṭṭho yen'attham sahasā naye,
yo ca attham anatthañ ca ubho niccheyya paṇḍito—

257. Asāhasena dhammena samena nayatī pare,
dhammassa gutto medhāvī dhammaṭṭho ti pavuccati.

256–257. Not by passing arbitrary judgements does one become just; a wise person who investigates both right and wrong, who does not judge others arbitrarily but passes judgement impartially according to truth, a sagacious guardian of the law, is called just. [1-2]

258. Na tena paṇḍito hoti yāvatā bahu bhāsati,
khemī averī abhayo paṇḍito ti pavuccati.

258. One is not wise because one speaks much; one who is peaceable, friendly, and fearless is called wise. [3]

259. Na tāvatā dhammadharo yāvatā bahu bhāsati,
yo ca appam pi sutvāna dhammaṃ kāyena passati,
sa ve dhammadharo hoti yo dhammaṃ nappamajjati.

259. One is not versed in the Dhamma because one speaks much. One who, after hearing even a little Dhamma, does not neglect it but personally realizes its truth is truly versed in the Dhamma. [4]

260. Na tena thero hoti yen'assa palitaṃ siro,
paripakko vayo tassa moghajiṇṇo ti vuccati.

260. A monk is not an elder because his head is gray; he is but ripe in age, and is called one grown old in vain. [5]

261. Yamhi saccañ ca dhammo ca ahiṃsā saññamo damo,
sa ve vantamalo dhīro thero iti pavuccati

261. One in whom there is truthfulness and virtue, inoffensiveness, restraint, and self-mastery, who is free from defilements and wise—he is truly called an elder. [6]

262. Na vākkaraṇamattena vaññapokkharatāya vā
sādhurūpo naro hoti issukī maccharī saṭho.

262. Not by mere eloquence nor by bodily beauty does a person become refined, should he be jealous, selfish, and deceitful. [7]

263. Yassa c'etaṃ samucchinnaṃ mūlaghaccaṃ samūhataṃ,
sa vantadoso medhāvī sādhurūpo ti vuccati.

263. But he in whom these are wholly destroyed, uprooted and extinct, and who has cast out imperfection—that sagacious person is said to be refined. [8]

264. Na muṇḍakena samaṇo abbato alikaṃ bhaṇaṃ;
icchālobhasamāpanno samaṇo kiṃ bhavissati?

264. Not by shaven head does one who is undisciplined and untruthful become a recluse. How can one who is full of desire and greed be a recluse? [9]

265. Yo ca sameti pāpāni aṇuṃ thūlāni sabbaso,
samitattā hi pāpānaṃ samaṇo ti pavuccati.

265. One who wholly subdues evil both small and great is called a recluse, because he has overcome all evil.[21] [10]

266. Na tena bhikkhu hoti yāvatā bhikkhate pare;
vissaṃ dhammaṃ samādāya bhikkhu hoti na tāvatā.

266. He is not a monk just because he lives on other's alms. Not by adopting outward form does one become a true monk. [11]

267. Yo'dha puññañ ca pāpañ ca bāhetvā brahmacariyavā
saṅkhāya loke carati, sa ve bhikkhū ti vuccati.

---

21. This is an "edifying etymology" based on a pun in the Pāli that cannot be satisfactorily reproduced in English.

267. One here who lives the holy life and walks with understanding in this world, transcending both merit and demerit—he is truly called a monk. [12]

> 268. *Na monena munī hoti mūḷharūpo aviddasu;*
> *yo ca tulaṃ va paggayha varam ādāya paṇḍito—*
>
> 269. *Pāpāni parivajjeti, sa munī tena so munī;*
> *yo munāti ubho loke munī tena pavuccati.*

268–269. Not by observing silence does one become a sage, if one is foolish and ignorant. But that wise person who, as if holding a balance-scale, accepts only the good and rejects the evil—he is truly a sage. Since he comprehends both (the present and future) worlds, he is called a sage. [13-14]

> 270. *Na tena ariyo hoti yena pāṇāni hiṃsati;*
> *ahiṃsā sabbapāṇānaṃ ariyo ti pavuccati.*

270. He is not a noble one who injures living beings. He is called a noble one because he is harmless towards all living beings. [15]

> 271. *Na sīlabbatamattena bāhusaccena vā puna*
> *atha vā samādhilābhena viviccasayanena vā—*
>
> 272. *Phusāmi nekkhammasukhaṃ aputhujjanasevitaṃ,*
> *bhikkhu vissāsa māpādi appatto āsavakkhayaṃ.*

271–272. Not with mere rules and observances, nor even with much learning, nor with the gain of absorption, nor with a life of seclusion, nor with thinking, "I enjoy the bliss of renunciation, which is not experienced by the worldling," should you rest content, O monks, so long as the utter destruction of cankers has not been reached. [16-17]

20

Maggavagga

The Path

273. Maggān'aṭṭhaṅgiko seṭṭho, saccānaṃ caturo padā,
virāgo seṭṭho dhammānaṃ, dipadānañ ca cakkhumā.

273. Of all paths the Eightfold Path is the best; of all truths the Four Noble Truths are the best; of all things passionlessness is the best; of humans, the Seeing One (the Buddha) is the best. [1]

274. Eso va maggo natth'añño, dassanassa visuddhiyā,
etamhi tumhe paṭipajjatha: mārass'etaṃ pamohanaṃ.

274. This is the only way: there is none other for the purification of insight. Tread this path, and you will bewilder Māra. [2]

275. Etamhi tumhe paṭipannā dukkhass'antaṃ karissatha,
akkhāto ve mayā maggo aññāya sallasanthanaṃ.

275. Walking upon this path you will make an end of suffering. Having discovered how to pull out the thorn of lust, I expound the path. [3]

276. Tumhehi kiccaṃ ātappaṃ akkhātāro Tathāgatā;
paṭipannā pamokkhanti jhāyino Mārabandhanā.

276. You yourselves must strive; the Tathāgatas only point the way. Those meditative ones who tread the path are released from the bonds of Māra.[22] [4]

277. Sabbe saṅkhārā aniccā ti yadā paññāya passati,
atha nibbindati dukkhe; esa maggo visuddhiyā.

---

22. Tathāgata: an epithet of the Buddha meaning "the Thus Come One" or "the Thus Gone One." The commentaries give elaborate explanations of the word.

277. "All conditioned things are impermanent"—when one sees this with wisdom one turns away from suffering. This is the path to purification. [5]

> *278. Sabbe saṅkhārā dukkhā ti yadā paññāya passati,*
> *atha nibbindati dukkhe; esa maggo visuddhiyā.*

278. "All conditioned things are unsatisfactory"—when one sees this with wisdom one turns away from suffering. This is the path to purification. [6]

> *279. Sabbe dhammā anattā ti yadā paññāya passati,*
> *atha nibbindati dukkhe; esa maggo visuddhiyā.*

279. "All things are not self"—when one sees this with wisdom one turns away from suffering. This is the path to purification. [7]

> *280. Uṭṭhānakālamhi anuṭṭhahāno yuvā balī ālasiyaṃ upeto,*
> *saṃsannasaṅkappamano kusīto paññāya maggaṃ alaso na vindati.*

280. The idler who does not exert himself when he should, who though young and strong is full of sloth, with a mind full of vain thoughts—such an indolent man does not find the path to wisdom. [8]

> *281. Vācānurakkhī manasā susaṃvuto, kāyena ca akusalaṃ na kayirā;*
> *ete tayo kammapathe visodhaye ārādhaye maggaṃ isippaveditaṃ.*

281. Watchful of speech, well controlled in mind, one should not commit evil with the body. Let one purify these three courses of action, and win the path made known by the Great Sage. [9]

> *282. Yogā ve jāyatī bhūri ayogā bhūrisaṅkhayo;*
> *etaṃ dvedhāpathaṃ ñatvā bhavāya vibhavāya ca,*
> *tath'attānaṃ niveseyya yathā bhūri pavaḍḍhati.*

282. Wisdom springs from meditation, without meditation wisdom wanes. Having known these two paths of progress and decline, one should so conduct oneself that wisdom increases. [10]

> *283. Vanaṃ chindatha mā rukkhaṃ, vanato jāyate bhayaṃ;*
> *chetvā vanañ ca vanathañ ca nibbanā hotha bhikkhavo.*

283. Cut down the forest (of lust), but not the tree. From the forest (of lust) springs fear. Having cut down the forest and the underbrush (of desire), be passionless, O monks![23] [11]

> *284. Yāva hi vanatho na chijjati aṇumatto pi narassa nārisu*
> *paṭibaddhamano va tāva so vaccho khīrapako va mātari.*

284. For so long as the underbrush of desire, even the most subtle, of a man towards a woman is not cut down, his mind is in bondage, like the sucking calf to its mother. [12]

> *285. Ucchinda sineham attano kumudaṃ sāradikaṃ va pāṇinā*
> *santimaggam eva brūhaya nibbānaṃ sugatena desitaṃ.*

285. Cut off your affection as one plucks with the hand an autumn lotus. Cultivate only the path to peace, to Nibbāna, as made known by the Exalted One. [13]

> *286. Idha vassaṃ vasissāmi idha hemantagimhisu*
> *iti bālo vicinteti antarāyaṃ na bujjhati.*

286. "Here shall I live during the rains, here in winter and summer"—thus thinks the fool. He does not realize the danger (that death might intervene). [14]

> *287. Taṃ puttapasusammattaṃ byāsattamanasaṃ naraṃ*
> *suttaṃ gāmaṃ mahogho va maccu ādāya gacchati.*

---

23. The meaning of this injunction is: "Cut down the forest of lust, but do not mortify the body."

287. As a great flood carries away a sleeping village, just so Death seizes and carries away a man with a grasping mind, doting on his children and cattle. [15]

> *288. Na santi puttā tāṇāya na pitā n'āpi bandhavā,*
> *antakenādhipannassa natthi ñātīsu tāṇatā.*

288. For one who is assailed by the Destroyer there is no protection by kinsmen. None there are to save him—no sons, nor father, nor relatives. [16]

> *289. Etam atthavasaṃ ñatvā paṇḍito sīlasaṃvuto*
> *nibbānagamanaṃ maggaṃ khippam eva visodhaye.*

289. Realizing this fact, let the wise man, restrained by morality, hasten to clear the path leading to Nibbāna. [17]

21

Pakiṇṇakavagga

Miscellaneous

290. Mattāsukhapariccāgā passe ce vipulaṃ sukhaṃ,
caje mattāsukhaṃ dhīro sampassaṃ vipulaṃ sukhaṃ.

290. If by renouncing a lesser happiness one may realize a greater happiness, let the wise man renounce the lesser, having regard for the greater happiness. [1]

291. Paradukkhūpadānena attano sukham icchati,
verasaṃsaggasaṃsaṭṭho verā so na parimuccati.

291. One who seeks his own happiness by inflicting pain on others, entangled by the bonds of hate, will never be delivered from hate. [2]

292. Yaṃ hi kiccaṃ tadapaviddhaṃ, akiccaṃ pana kayirati;
unnaḷānaṃ pamattānaṃ tesaṃ vaḍḍhanti āsavā.

292. For those who are arrogant and heedless, who leave undone what should be done and do what should not be done—for them the cankers only increase. [3]

293. Yesañ ca susamāraddhā niccaṃ kāyagatā sati,
akiccaṃ te na sevanti kicce sātaccakārino,
satānaṃ sampajānānaṃ atthaṃ gacchanti āsavā.

293. Those who always earnestly practise mindfulness of the body, who do not resort to what should not be done, and steadfastly pursue what should be done, mindful and clearly comprehending—their cankers come to an end. [4]

294. Mātaraṃ pitaraṃ hantvā rājāno dve ca khattiye
raṭṭhaṃ sānucaraṃ hantvā anīgho yāti brāhmaṇo.

294. Having slain mother (craving), father (ego-conceit), two warrior kings (eternalism and nihilism), and destroyed a country

(sense organs and sense objects) together with its treasurer (attachment and lust), ungrieving goes the holy man. [5]

295. Mātaraṃ pitaraṃ hantvā rājāno dve ca sotthiye
veyyagghapañcamaṃ hantvā anīgho yāti brāhmaṇo.

295. Having slain mother, father, two brahmin kings (two extreme views), and a tiger as the fifth (the five mental hindrances), ungrieving goes the holy man. [6]

296. Suppabuddhaṃ pabujjhanti sadā Gotamasāvakā,
yesaṃ divā ca ratto ca niccaṃ Buddhagatā sati.

296. Those disciples of Gotama ever awaken happily who day and night constantly practise the recollection of the Buddha. [7]

297. Suppabuddhaṃ pabujjhanti sadā Gotamasāvakā,
yesaṃ divā ca ratto ca niccaṃ dhammagatā sati.

297. Those disciples of Gotama ever awaken happily who day and night constantly practise the recollection of the Dhamma. [8]

298. Suppabuddhaṃ pabujjhanti sadā Gotamasāvakā,
yesaṃ divā ca ratto ca niccaṃ saṅghagatā sati.

298. Those disciples of Gotama ever awaken happily who day and night constantly practise the recollection of the Sangha. [9]

299. Suppabuddhaṃ pabujjhanti sadā Gotamasāvakā,
yesaṃ divā ca ratto ca niccaṃ kāyagatā sati.

299. Those disciples of Gotama ever awaken happily who day and night constantly practise mindfulness of the body. [10]

300. Suppabuddhaṃ pabujjhanti sadā Gotamasāvakā,
yesaṃ divā ca ratto ca ahiṃsāya rato mano.

300. Those disciples of Gotama ever awaken happily whose minds by day and night delight in the practice of non-harming. [11]

301. Suppabuddhaṃ pabujjhanti sadā Gotamasāvakā,
yesaṃ divā ca ratto ca bhāvanāya rato mano.

301. Those disciples of Gotama ever awaken happily whose minds by day and night delight in the practice of meditation. [12]

302. Duppabbajjaṃ durabhiramaṃ, durāvāsā gharā dukhā,
dukkho'samānasaṃvāso, dukkhānupatit'addhagū;
tasmā na c'addhagū siyā, dukkhānupatito siyā.

302. Difficult is life as a monk; difficult is it to delight therein. Also difficult and sorrowful is household life. Suffering comes from association with unequals, suffering comes from aimless wandering (in saṃsāra). Therefore, do not be an aimless wanderer, a pursuer of suffering. [13]

303. Saddho sīlena sampanno yasobhogasamappito
yaṃ yaṃ padesaṃ bhajati tattha tatth'eva pūjito.

303. He who is full of faith and virtue, and who possesses good repute and wealth—he is respected everywhere, in whatever land he travels. [14]

304. Dūre santo pakāsenti Himavanto va pabbato,
asant'ettha na dissanti rattikhittā yathā sarā.

304. The good shine even from afar, like the Himalaya mountains. But the wicked are unseen, like arrows shot in the night. [15]

305. Ekāsanaṃ ekaseyyaṃ eko caram atandito
eko damayaṃ attānaṃ vanante ramito siyā.

305. He who sits alone, sleeps alone, and walks alone, who is strenuous and subdues himself alone, will find delight in the solitude of the forest. [16]

22
Nirayavagga
Hell

306. Abhūtavādī nirayaṃ upeti yo vā pi katvā na karomī ti c'āha;
ubho pi te pecca samā bhavanti nihīnakammā manujā parattha.

306. The false accuser goes to hell; also one who, having done (wrong), says "I did not do it." Men of base actions both, on departing they share the same destiny in the other world.[24] [1]

307. Kāsāvakaṇṭhā bahavo pāpadhammā asaññatā
pāpā pāpehi kammehi nirayaṃ te upapajjare.

307. There are many uncontrolled men of evil character wearing the yellow robe. These wicked men will be reborn in hell because of their evil deeds. [2]

308. Seyyo ayoguḷo bhutto tatto aggisikhūpamo,
yañ ce bhuñjeyya dussīlo raṭṭhapiṇḍaṃ asaññato.

308. It would be better to swallow a red-hot iron ball, blazing like fire, than as an immoral and uncontrolled monk to eat the almsfood of the people. [3]

309. Cattāri ṭhānāni naro pamatto āpajjati paradārūpasevī:
apuññalābhaṃ, na nikāmaseyyaṃ, nindaṃ tatīyaṃ, nirayaṃ catutthaṃ.

309. Four misfortunes befall the reckless man who consorts with another's wife: acquisition of demerit, disturbed sleep, ill-repute, and (rebirth in) hell. [4]

---

24. The false accuser (*abhūtavādī*): the commentary explains as "one who, without having seen the fault of another, by speaking falsehood groundlessly maligns him."

310. Apuññalābho ca gatī ca pāpikā, bhītassa bhītāya ratī ca thokikā,
rājā ca daṇḍaṃ garukaṃ paṇeti, tasmā naro paradāraṃ na seve.

310. Such a man acquires demerit and an unhappy birth in the future. Brief is the pleasure of the frightened man and woman, and the king imposes heavy punishment. Hence let no man consort with another's wife. [5]

311. Kuso yathā duggahīto hattham ev'ānukantati,
sāmaññaṃ dupparāmaṭṭhaṃ nirayāy'ūpakaḍḍhati.

311. Just as *kusa* grass wrongly handled cuts the hand, even so a recluse's life wrongly lived drags one to hell. [6]

312. Yaṃ kiñci sithilaṃ kammaṃ saṅkiliṭṭhañ ca yaṃ vataṃ
saṅkassaraṃ brahmacariyaṃ na taṃ hoti mahapphalaṃ.

312. Any loose act, any corrupt observance, any life of questionable celibacy—none of these bear much fruit. [7]

313. Kayirā ce kayirāth'enaṃ daḷham enaṃ parakkame;
sithilo hi paribbājo bhiyyo ākirate rajaṃ.

313. If anything is to be done, let one do it with sustained vigor. A lax monastic life stirs up the dust of passions all the more. [8]

314. Akataṃ dukkaṭaṃ seyyo, pacchā tappati dukkaṭaṃ,
katañ ca sukataṃ seyyo yaṃ katvā nānutappati.

314. An evil deed is better left undone, for such a deed torments one afterwards. But a good deed is better done, doing which one does not repent. [9]

315. Nagaraṃ yathā paccantaṃ guttaṃ santarabāhiraṃ,
evaṃ gopetha attānaṃ khaṇo ve mā upaccagā;
khaṇātītā hi socanti nirayamhi samappitā.

315. Guard yourself closely like a border city, both within and without. Do not let slip this opportunity (for spiritual growth). For those who let slip this opportunity grieve when consigned to hell. [10]

316. Alajjitāye lajjanti, lajjitāye na lajjare,
micchādiṭṭhisamādānā sattā gacchanti duggatiṃ.

316. Those who are ashamed of what they should not be ashamed of, and who are not ashamed of what they should be ashamed of—upholding false views, these people go to a state of woe. [11]

317. Abhaye bhayadassino, bhaye c'ābhayadassino,
micchādiṭṭhisamādānā sattā gacchanti duggatiṃ.

317. Those who see something to fear where there is nothing to fear, and who see nothing to fear where there is something to fear—upholding false views, these people go to a state of woe. [12]

318. Avajje vajjamatino, vajje c'āvajjadassino,
micchādiṭṭhisamādānā sattā gacchanti duggatiṃ.

318. Those who find fault in the faultless, and who find no fault in a fault—upholding wrong views, these people go to a state of woe. [13]

319. Vajjañ ca vajjato ñatvā, avajjañ ca avajjato,
sammādiṭṭhisamādānā sattā gacchanti suggatiṃ.

319. Having known a fault to be a fault and the faultless to be faultless—upholding right views, these people go to a happy realm. [14]

23

Nāgavagga

The Elephant

320. Ahaṃ nāgo va saṅgāme cāpāto patitaṃ saraṃ
ativākyaṃ titikkhissaṃ; dussīlo hi bahujjano.

320. As an elephant in battle withstands arrows shot from bows all around, even so will I endure abuse. There are many, indeed, who lack morality. [1]

321. Dantaṃ nayanti samitiṃ, dantaṃ rājā'bhirūhati,
danto seṭṭho manussesu yo'tivākyaṃ titikkhati.

321. A tamed elephant can be led into a crowd, and the king mounts a tamed elephant. So too, best among humans is the subdued one who endures abuse. [2]

322. Varam assatarā dantā, ājānīyā ca sindhavā,
kuñjarā ca mahānāgā, attadanto tato varaṃ.

322. Excellent are well-trained mules, thoroughbred Sindhu horses, and noble tusker elephants. But better still is one who has subdued himself. [3]

323. Na hi etehi yānehi gaccheyya agataṃ disaṃ,
yathā'ttanā sudantena danto dantena gacchati.

323. Not by these mounts, however, can one go to the untrodden land (Nibbāna), as one who is self-tamed goes by his own tamed and well-controlled mind. [4]

324. Dhanapālako nāma kuñjaro kaṭukappabhedano
dunnivārayo;
baddho kabalaṃ na bhuñjati, sumarati nāgavanassa
kuñjaro.

324. Musty during rut, the tusker named Dhanapālaka is uncontrollable. Held in captivity, the tusker does not touch a morsel, but only longingly calls to mind the elephant forest. [5]

> *325. Middhī yadā hoti mahagghaso ca niddāyitā samparivattasāyī*
> *mahāvarāho va nivāpapuṭṭho punappunaṃ gabbham upeti mando.*

325. When one is sluggish and gluttonous, lazy, rolling around in bed like a fat pig—that sluggard undergoes rebirth again and again. [6]

> *326. Idaṃ pure cittam acāri cārikaṃ yen'icchakaṃ yatthakāmaṃ yathāsukhaṃ,*
> *Tad ajj'ahaṃ niggahessāmi yoniso hatthippabhinnaṃ viya aṅkusaggaho.*

326. Formerly this mind wandered about as it liked, where it wished, according to its pleasure, but now I will thoroughly master it with wisdom, as a mahout controls an elephant in rut. [7]

> *327. Appamādaratā hotha, sacittam anurakkhatha,*
> *duggā uddharath'attānaṃ paṅke sanno va kuñjaro.*

327. Delight in heedfulness! Guard well your own mind! Draw yourself out of this bog of evil, even as an elephant draws himself out of the mud. [8]

> *328. Sace labhetha nipakaṃ sahāyaṃ saddhiñcaraṃ sādhuvihāridhīraṃ,*
> *abhibhuyya sabbāni parissayāni careyya ten'attamano satīmā.*

328. If for company you find a wise and prudent friend, one who leads a good life, you should overcome all impediments and keep his company, joyously and mindfully. [9]

329. No ce labhetha nipakaṃ sahāyaṃ saddhiñcaraṃ sādhuvihāridhīraṃ,
rājā va raṭṭhaṃ vijitaṃ pahāya eko care mātaṅgaraññe va nāgo.

329. But if for company you cannot find a wise and prudent friend, one who leads a good life, then, like a king who leaves behind a conquered kingdom or a lone elephant in the elephant forest, you should go your own way alone. [10]

330. Ekassa caritaṃ seyyo natthi bāle sahāyatā,
eko care na ca pāpāni kayirā appossukko mātaṅgaraññe va nāgo.

330. Better it is to live alone, there is no fellowship with a fool. Live alone and do no evil; be carefree like an elephant in the elephant forest. [11]

331. Atthamhi jātamhi sukhā sahāyā, tuṭṭhī sukhā yā itarītarena,
puññaṃ sukhaṃ jīvitasaṅkhayamhi, sabbassa dukkhassa sukhaṃ pahānaṃ.

331. Blessed are friends when need arises; blessed is contentment with just what one has; blessed is merit when life is at an end; and blessed is the abandoning of all suffering. [12]

332. Sukhā matteyyatā loke atho petteyyatā sukhā
sukhā sāmaññatā loke atho brahmaññatā sukhā.

332. Blessed it is to serve one's mother; blessed it is to serve one's father; blessed it is to serve the monks; and blessed it is to serve the holy men. [13]

333. Sukhaṃ yāva jarā sīlaṃ sukhā saddhā patiṭṭhitā
sukho paññāya paṭilābho pāpānaṃ akaraṇaṃ sukhaṃ.

333. Blessed is virtue until life's end; blessed is faith that is steadfast; blessed is the acquisition of wisdom; and blessed is the avoidance of evil. [14]

24

Taṇhāvagga

Craving

334. Manujassa pamattacārino taṇhā vaḍḍhati māluvā viya,
so plavati hurāhuraṃ phalam icchaṃ va vanasmiṃ vānaro.

334. The craving of a person given to heedless living grows like a creeper. Like the monkey seeking fruits in the forest, he leaps from life to life (tasting the fruit of his kamma). [1]

335. Yaṃ esā sahate jammī taṅhā loke visattikā
sokā tassa pavaḍḍhanti abhivaṭṭhaṃ va bīraṇaṃ.

335. Whoever is overcome by this wretched and sticky craving, his sorrows grow like *bīraṇa* grass after the rains. [2]

336. Yo c'etaṃ sahate jammiṃ taṇhaṃ loke duraccayaṃ
sokā tamhā papatanti udabindū va pokkharā.

336. But whoever overcomes this wretched craving, so difficult to overcome, from him sorrows fall away like water from a lotus leaf. [3]

337. Taṃ vo vadāmi bhaddaṃ vo, yāvant'ettha samāgatā,
taṇhāya mūlaṃ khaṇatha usīrattho va bīraṇaṃ;
mā vo naḷaṃ va soto va Māro bhañji punappunaṃ.

337. This I say to you: Good luck to you all assembled here! Dig up the root of craving, like one in search of the fragrant roots of *bīraṇa* grass. Do not let Māra crush you again and again, as a flood crushes a reed. [4]

338. Yathāpi mūle anupaddave daḷhe chinno pi rukkho punar eva rūhati,
evam pi taṇhānusaye anūhate nibbattatī dukkham idaṃ punappunaṃ.

338. Just as a tree, though cut down, sprouts up again if its roots remain uncut and firm, even so, until the craving that lies dormant is rooted out, this suffering springs up again and again. [5]

> *339. Yassa chattiṃsatī sotā manāpasavanā bhusā*
> *vāhā vahanti duddiṭṭhiṃ saṅkappā rāganissitā.*

339. The misguided person, in whom the thirty-six currents of craving rush strongly toward pleasurable objects, is swept away by the flood of passionate thoughts.[25] [6]

> *340. Savanti sabbadhī sotā, latā ubbhijja tiṭṭhati,*
> *tañ ca disvā lataṃ jātaṃ mūlaṃ paññāya chindatha.*

340. Everywhere these currents flow, and the creeper (of craving) sprouts and grows. Seeing that the creeper has sprung up, cut off its root with wisdom. [7]

> *341. Saritāni sinehitāni ca somanassāni bhavanti jantuno,*
> *te sātasitā sukhesino te ve jātijarūpagā narā.*

341. Flowing in (from all objects) and watered by craving, feelings of pleasure arise in beings. Bent on pleasure and seeking enjoyment, these people fall prey to birth and decay. [8]

> *342. Tasiṇāya purakkhatā pajā parisappanti saso va bandhito,*
> *saññojanasaṅgasattakā dukkham upenti punappunaṃ*
> *cirāya.*

342. Beset by craving, people run about like an entrapped hare. Held fast by mental fetters, they come to suffering again and again for a long time. [9]

25. The thirty-six currents of craving: the three cravings—for sensual pleasure, for continued existence, and for annihilation—in relation to each of the twelve sense bases: the six sense organs, including mind, and their corresponding objects.

343. Tasiṇāya purakkhatā pajā parisappanti saso va bandhito,
tasmā tasiṇaṃ vinodaye ākaṅkhanta virāgam attano.

343. Beset by craving, people run about like an entrapped hare. Therefore one who yearns to be passion-free should destroy his own craving. [10]

344. Yo nibbanatho vanādhimutto vanamutto vanam eva dhāvati,
taṃ puggalam etha passatha, mutto bandhanam eva dhāvati.

344. There is one who had turned away from the forest (of desire), intent on the life of the forest (as a monk). But after being freed from the forest (of desire), he runs back to that same forest. Come, behold that man! Though freed, he runs back to that very bondage.[26] [11]

345. Na taṃ daḷhaṃ bandhanam āhu dhīrā yad āyasaṃ dārujaṃ babbajañ ca;
sārattarattā maṇikuṇḍalesu, puttesu dāresu ca yā apekkhā—

346. Etaṃ daḷhaṃ bandhanam āhu dhīrā ohārinaṃ sithilaṃ duppamuñcaṃ;
etam pi chetvāna paribbajanti anapekkhino kāmasukhaṃ pahāya.

345–346. That is not a strong fetter, the wise say, which is made of iron, wood, or hemp. But the infatuation and longing for jewels and ornaments, for children and wives—that, the wise say, is a far stronger fetter, which pulls one downward and, though seemingly loose, is hard to remove. This too the wise cut off. Giving up sensual pleasure, and without any longing, they renounce the world. [12-13]

---

26. This verse, in the original, puns with the Pāli word *vana*, meaning both "desire" and "forest." According to the commentary, this verse was spoken with reference to a renegade monk.

347. Ye rāgarattānupatanti sotaṃ sayaṃkataṃ makkaṭako va jālaṃ,
etampi chetvāna vajanti dhīrā anapekkhino sabbadukkhaṃ pahāya.

347. Those who are lust-infatuated fall back to the swirling current (of saṃsāra) like a spider on its self-spun web. This too the wise cut off. Without any longing, they abandon all suffering and renounce the world. [14]

348. Muñca pure muñca pacchato majjhe muñca bhavassa pāragū,
sabbattha vimuttamānaso na puna jātijaraṃ upehisi.

348. Let go of the past, let go of the future, let go of the present, and cross over to the farther shore of existence. With mind wholly liberated, you shall come no more to birth and decay. [15]

349. Vitakkapamathitassa jantuno tibbarāgassa subhānupassino
bhiyyo taṇhā pavaḍḍhati, esa kho daḷhaṃ karoti bandhanaṃ.

349. For a person tormented by evil thoughts, who is passion-dominated and given to the pursuit of pleasure, his craving steadily grows. He makes the fetter strong indeed. [16]

350. Vitakkūpasame ca yo rato asubhaṃ bhāvayati sadā sato,
esa kho vyantikāhiti, esa checchati Mārabandhanaṃ.

350. He who delights in subduing evil thoughts, who meditates on the impurities and is ever mindful—it is he who will make an end of craving and rend asunder Māra's fetter. [17]

351. Niṭṭhaṅgato asantāsī vītataṇho anaṅgaṇo
acchindi bhavasallāni antimo'yaṃ samussayo.

351. He who has reached the goal, fearless, free from craving, stainless, having plucked out the thorns of existence—for him this is the last body. [18]

352. Vītataṇho anādāno niruttipadakovido
akkharānaṃ sannipātaṃ jaññā pubbāparāni ca,
sa ve antimasārīro mahāpañño mahāpuriso ti vuccati.

352. He who is free from craving and attachment, perfect in uncovering the true meaning of the Teaching, and who knows the arrangement of the sacred texts in correct sequence—he, indeed, is the bearer of his final body. He is truly called a profoundly wise one, a great man. [19]

353. Sabbābhibhū sabbavidū'ham asmi sabbesu dhammesu anūpalitto
sabbañjaho taṇhakkhaye vimutto, sayaṃ abhiññāya kam uddiseyyaṃ?

353. A victor am I over all, all have I known, yet unattached am I to all that is conquered and known. Abandoning all, I am freed through the destruction of craving. Having thus directly comprehended all by myself, whom shall I call my teacher?[27] [20]

354. Sabbadānaṃ dhammadānaṃ jināti, sabbaṃ rasaṃ dhammaraso jināti,
sabbaṃ ratiṃ dhammaratī jināti, taṇhakkhayo sabbadukkhaṃ jināti.

354. The gift of the Dhamma excels all gifts; the taste of the Dhamma excels all tastes; the delight in the Dhamma excels all delights; the craving-freed vanquishes all suffering. [21]

355. Hananti bhogā dummedhaṃ no ca pāragavesino
bhogataṇhāya dummedho hanti aññe va attanaṃ.

355. Riches ruin the foolish, but not those in quest of the Beyond. By craving for riches the witless man ruins himself as well as others. [22]

---

27. This was the Buddha's reply to a wandering ascetic who asked him about his teacher. The Buddha's answer shows that his Enlightenment was his own unique discovery, which he had not learned from anyone else.

356. Tiṇadosāni khettāni, rāgadosā ayaṃ pajā,
tasmā hi vītarāgesu dinnaṃ hoti mahapphalaṃ.

356. Weeds are the bane of fields, lust the bane of humankind. Therefore what is offered to those free of lust yields abundant fruit. [23]

357. Tiṇadosāni khettāni, dosadosā ayaṃ pajā,
tasmā hi vītadosesu dinnaṃ hoti mahapphalaṃ.

357. Weeds are the bane of fields, hatred the bane of humankind. Therefore what is offered to those free of hatred yields abundant fruit. [24]

358. Tiṇadosāni khettāni, mohadosā ayaṃ pajā,
tasmā hi vītamohesu dinnaṃ hoti mahapphalaṃ.

358. Weeds are the bane of fields, delusion the bane of humankind. Therefore what is offered to those free of delusion yields abundant fruit. [25]

359. Tiṇadosāni khettāni, icchādosā ayaṃ pajā,
tasmā hi vigaticchesu dinnaṃ hoti mahapphalaṃ.

359. Weeds are the bane of fields, desire the bane of humankind. Therefore what is offered to those free of desire yields abundant fruit. [26]

25

Bhikkhuvagga

The Monk

360. Cakkhunā saṃvaro sādhu, sādhu sotena saṃvaro,
ghānena saṃvaro sādhu, sādhu jivhāya saṃvaro.

360. Good is restraint over the eye; good is restraint over the ear; good is restraint over the nose; good is restraint over the tongue. [1]

361. Kāyena saṃvaro sādhu, sādhu vācāya saṃvaro,
manasā saṃvaro sādhu, sādhu sabbattha saṃvaro;
sabbattha saṃvuto bhikkhu sabbadukkhā pamuccati.

361. Good is restraint in the body; good is restraint in speech; good is restraint in thought. Restraint everywhere is good. The monk restrained in every way is freed from all suffering. [2]

362. Hatthasaññato pādasaññato vācāya saññato
saññatuttamo
ajjhattarato samāhito eko santusito tam āhu bhikkhuṃ.

362. He who has control over his hands, feet, and tongue, who is fully controlled, delights in meditation, is inwardly absorbed, keeps to himself and is contented—him do people call a monk. [3]

363. Yo mukhasaññato bhikkhu mantabhāṇī anuddhato
atthaṃ dhammañ ca dīpeti, madhuraṃ tassa bhāsitaṃ.

363. That monk who has control over his tongue, is moderate in speech, unassuming and who explains the Teaching in both letter and spirit—whatever he says is pleasing. [4]

364. Dhammārāmo dhammarato dhammaṃ anuvicintayaṃ
dhammaṃ anussaraṃ bhikkhu saddhammā na
parihāyati.

364. The monk who abides in the Dhamma, delights in the Dhamma, meditates on the Dhamma, and bears the Dhamma well in mind—he does not fall away from the sublime Dhamma. [5]

365. Salābhaṃ nātimaññeyya, nāññesaṃ pihayaṃ care;
aññesaṃ pihayaṃ bhikkhu samādhiṃ nādhigacchati.

365. One should not despise what one has received, nor envy the gains of others. The monk who envies the gains of others does not attain to meditative absorption. [6]

366. Appalābho pi ce bhikkhu salābhaṃ nātimaññati,
taṃ ve devā pasaṃsanti suddhājīviṃ atanditaṃ.

366. If a monk does not despise what he has received, even though it be little, if he is pure in livelihood and unremitting in effort, even the gods praise him. [7]

367. Sabbaso nāmarūpasmiṃ yassa natthi mamāyitaṃ,
asatā ca na socati, sa ve bhikkhū ti vuccati.

367. He who has no attachment whatsoever for the mind and body, who does not grieve for what he has not—he is truly called a monk. [8]

368. Mettāvihārī yo bhikkhu pasanno Buddhasāsane
adhigacche padaṃ santaṃ saṅkhārūpasamaṃ sukhaṃ.

368. The monk who abides in universal love and is deeply devoted to the Teaching of the Buddhas attains the peace of Nibbāna, the bliss of the cessation of conditioned things. [9]

369. Siñca bhikkhu imaṃ nāvaṃ, sittā te lahum essati,
chetvā rāgañ ca dosañ ca tato nibbānam ehisi.

369. Empty this boat, O monk! Emptied, it will sail lightly. Having cut off lust and hatred, you shall reach Nibbāna. [10]

370. Pañca chinde pañca jahe, pañca c'uttari bhāvaye;
pañcasaṅgātigo bhikkhu oghatiṇṇo ti vuccati.

370. Cut off the five, abandon the five, and cultivate the five. The monk who has overcome the five bonds is called one who has crossed the flood.[28] [11]

> *371. Jhāya bhikkhu mā ca pamādo, mā te kāmaguṇe bhamassu cittaṃ,*
> *mā lohaguḷaṃ gilī pamatto, mā kandi 'dukkham idan' ti ḍayhamāno.*

371. Meditate, O monk! Do not be heedless. Do not let your mind whirl on sensual pleasures. Heedless, do not swallow a red hot iron ball, lest you cry when burning, "Oh, this is painful!" [12]

> *372. Natthi jhānaṃ apaññassa, paññā natthi ajjhāyato,*
> *yamhi jhānañ ca paññā ca sa ve nibbānasantike.*

372. There is no meditative concentration for one who lacks wisdom, and no wisdom for one who lacks meditative concentration. One in whom are found both meditative concentration and wisdom is indeed close to Nibbāna. [13]

> *373. Suññāgāraṃ paviṭṭhassa santacittassa bhikkhuno,*
> *amānusī ratī hoti sammā dhammaṃ vipassato.*

373. When a monk who has retired to a solitary abode and calmed his mind comprehends the Dhamma with insight, there arises in him a delight that transcends all human delights. [14]

> *374. Yato yato sammasati khandhānaṃ udayabbayaṃ,*
> *labhatī pītipāmojjaṃ, amataṃ taṃ vijānataṃ.*

---

28. The five to be cut off are the five "lower fetters": self-illusion, doubt, belief in rites and rituals, lust, and ill-will. The five to be abandoned are the five "higher fetters": craving for the divine realms with form, craving for the formless realms, conceit, restlessness, and ignorance. Stream-enterers and once-returners cut off the first three fetters, non-returners the first five, and arahats all ten. The five to be cultivated are the five spiritual faculties: faith, energy, mindfulness, concentration, and wisdom. The five bonds are greed, hatred, delusion, false views, and conceit.

374. Whenever he sees with insight the rise and fall of the aggregates, he is full of joy and happiness. To the discerning, this reflects the Deathless.[29] [15]

> *375. Tatrāyam ādi bhavati idha paññassa bhikkhuno,*
> *indriyagutti santuṭṭhi, pātimokkhe ca saṃvaro.*

375. Control of the senses, contentment, restraint according to the code of monastic discipline—these form the basis of the holy life for the wise monk here. [16]

> *376. Mitte bhajassu kalyāṇe, suddhājīve atandite,*
> *paṭisanthāravutyassa, ācārakusalo siyā,*
> *tato pāmojjabahulo dukkhass'antaṃ karissati.*

376. Let him associate with friends who are noble, energetic, and pure in life; let him be cordial and refined in conduct. Thus, full of joy, he will make an end of suffering. [17]

> *377. Vassikā viya pupphāni maddavāni pamuñcati,*
> *evaṃ rāgañ ca dosañ ca vippamuñcetha bhikkhavo.*

377. Just as the jasmine creeper sheds its withered flowers, even so, O monks, should you totally shed lust and hatred! [18]

> *378. Santakāyo santavāco santavā susamāhito*
> *vantalokāmiso bhikkhu upasanto ti vuccati.*

378. The monk who is calm in body, calm in speech, calm in thought, well composed and who has spewn out worldliness—he, truly, is called serene. [19]

> *379. Attanā coday'attānaṃ, paṭimaṃsetha attanā,*
> *so attagutto satimā sukhaṃ bhikkhu vihāhisi.*

379. By oneself one must censure oneself and scrutinize oneself. The self-guarded and mindful monk will always live in happiness. [20]

---

29. See note 19.

380. Attā hi attano nātho, attā hi attano gati,
tasmā saññamay'attānaṃ assaṃ bhadraṃ va vāṇijo.

380. One is truly one's own protector; one is truly one's own refuge. Therefore one should control oneself even as the trader controls a noble steed. [21]

381. Pāmojjabahulo bhikkhu pasanno Buddhasāsane
adhigacche padaṃ santaṃ saṅkhārūpasamaṃ sukhaṃ.

381. Full of joy, full of faith in the Teaching of the Buddha, the monk attains the peaceful state, the bliss of cessation of conditioned things. [22]

382. Yo have daharo bhikkhu yuñjati Buddhasāsane
so imaṃ lokaṃ pabhāseti abbhā mutto va candimā.

382. That monk who while young devotes himself to the Teaching of the Buddha illuminates this world like the moon freed from a cloud. [23]

26

Brāhmaṇavagga
The Holy Man

383. Chinda sotaṃ parakkamma, kāme panuda brāhmaṇa,
saṅkhārānaṃ khayaṃ ñatvā akataññū'si brāhmaṇa.

383. Exert yourself and cut off the stream (of craving)! Discard sense desires, O holy man! Having known the destruction of conditioned things, become a knower of the Uncreate (Nibbāna), O holy man.[30] [1]

384. Yadā dvayesu dhammesu pāragū hoti brāhmaṇo,
ath'assa sabbe saṃyogā atthaṃ gacchanti jānato.

384. When a holy man has reached the summit of the two paths (meditative concentration and insight), he knows the truth and all his fetters fall away. [2]

385. Yassa pāram apāraṃ vā pārāpāraṃ na vijjati,
vītaddaraṃ visaṃyuttaṃ, tam ahaṃ brūmi brāhmaṇaṃ.

385. He for whom there is neither this shore nor the other shore, nor yet both, he who is free of cares and is unfettered—him do I call a holy man.[31] [3]

---

30. "Holy man" is used as a makeshift rendering for brāhmaṇa, intended to reproduce the ambiguity of the Indian word. Originally men of spiritual stature, by the time of the Buddha the brahmins had turned into a privileged priesthood which defined itself by means of birth and lineage rather than by genuine inner sanctity. The Buddha attempted to restore to the word brāhmaṇa its original connotation by identifying the true "holy man" as the arahat, who merits the title through his inward purity and holiness regardless of family lineage. The contrast between the two meanings is highlighted in vv.393 and 396. Those who led a contemplative life dedicated to gaining arahatship could also be called brahmins, as in vv.383, 389, and 390.

31. This shore: the six sense organs; the other shore: their corresponding objects; both: I-ness and my-ness.

386. Jhāyiṃ virajam āsīnaṃ katakiccaṃ anāsavaṃ
uttamatthaṃ anuppattaṃ tam ahaṃ brūmi brāhmaṇaṃ.

386. He who is meditative and stainless, settled and whose work is done, free from cankers, having reached the highest goal—him do I call a holy man. [4]

387. Divā tapati ādicco, rattiṃ ābhāti candimā;
sannaddho khattiyo tapati, jhāyī tapati brāhmaṇo,
atha sabbam ahorattiṃ Buddho tapati tejasā.

387. The sun shines by day, the moon shines by night. The warrior shines in armour, the holy man shines in meditation. But the Buddha shines resplendent all day and all night. [5]

388. Bāhitapāpo ti brāhmaṇo, samacariyā samaṇo ti vuccati;
pabbājay'attano malaṃ, tasmā pabbajito ti vuccati.

388. Because he has discarded evil, he is called a holy man. Because he is serene in conduct, he is called a recluse. And because he has renounced his own impurities, he is called a renunciate.[32] [6]

389. Na brāhmaṇassa pahareyya, nāssa muñcetha brāhmaṇo,
dhī brāhmaṇassa hantāraṃ tato dhī yassa muñcati.

389. One should not strike a holy man, nor should a holy man, when struck, give way to anger. Shame on him who strikes a holy man, and more shame on him who gives way to anger. [7]

390. Na brāhmaṇass'etad akiñci seyyo yadā nisedho manaso piyehi
yato yato hiṃsamano nivattati tato tato sammati-m-eva dukkhaṃ.

390. Nothing is better for a holy man than when he holds his mind back from what is endearing. To the extent that thoughts of harming wear away, to that extent does suffering subside. [8]

---

32. These are "edifying etymologies" based on puns in the Pāli.

391. Yassa kāyena vācāya manasā natthi dukkaṭaṃ
saṃvutaṃ tīhi ṭhānehi tam ahaṃ brūmi brāhmaṇaṃ.

391. He who does no evil in deed, word, and thought, who is restrained in these three ways—him do I call a holy man. [9]

392. Yamhā dhammaṃ vijāneyya sammāsambuddhadesitaṃ
sakkaccaṃ taṃ namasseyya aggihuttaṃ va brāhmaṇo.

392. Just as a brahmin priest reveres his sacrificial fire, even so should one devoutly revere the person from whom one has learned the Dhamma taught by the Supreme Buddha. [10]

393. Na jaṭāhi na gottena na jaccā hoti brāhmaṇo,
yamhi saccañ ca dhammo ca so sucī so ca brāhmaṇo.

393. Not by matted hair, nor by lineage, nor by birth does one become a holy man. But he in whom truth and righteousness exist—he is pure, he is a holy man. [11]

394. Kiṃ te jaṭāhi dummedha? kiṃ te ajinasāṭiyā?
Abbhantaraṃ te gahanaṃ bāhiraṃ parimajjasi.

394. What is the use of your matted hair, O witless man? What of your garment of antelope's hide? Within you is the tangle (of passion), only outwardly do you cleanse yourself.[33] [12]

395. Paṃsukūladharaṃ jantuṃ kisaṃ dhamanisanthataṃ,
ekaṃ vanasmiṃ jhāyantaṃ tam ahaṃ brūmi brāhmaṇaṃ.

395. The person who wears a robe made from rags, who is lean, with veins showing all over the body, and who meditates alone in the forest—him do I call a holy man. [13]

396. Na c'āhaṃ brāhmaṇaṃ brūmi yonijaṃ
mattisambhavaṃ,
bhovādī nāma so hoti sa ce hoti sakiñcano;
akiñcanaṃ anādānaṃ tam ahaṃ brūmi brāhmaṇaṃ.

33. In the time of the Buddha, as also still today in India, such ascetic practices as wearing matted hair and garments of hides were considered marks of holiness.

396. I do not call him a holy man because of his lineage or his high-born mother. If he has impeding attachments, he is just a supercilious man. But he who is free from impediments and clinging—him do I call a holy man. [14]

397. Sabbasaññojanaṃ chetvā yo ve na paritassati,
saṅgātigaṃ visaṃyuttaṃ tam ahaṃ brūmi brāhmaṇaṃ.

397. He who, having cut off all fetters, trembles no more, who has overcome all attachments and is emancipated—him do I call a holy man. [15]

398. Chetvā naddhiṃ varattañ ca sandāmaṃ sahanukkamaṃ,
ukkhittapaḷighaṃ buddhaṃ tam ahaṃ brūmi brāhmaṇaṃ.

398. He who has cut off the thong (of hatred), the band (of craving), and the rope (of false views), together with the appurtenances (latent evil tendencies), he who has removed the crossbar (ignorance) and is enlightened—him do I call a holy man. [16]

399. Akkosaṃ vadhabandhañ ca aduṭṭho yo titikkhati,
khantībalaṃ balānīkaṃ tam ahaṃ brūmi brāhmaṇaṃ.

399. He who without resentment endures abuse, beating, and punishment, whose power, real might, is patience—him do I call a holy man. [17]

400. Akkodhanaṃ vatavantaṃ sīlavantaṃ anussutaṃ
dantaṃ antimasārīraṃ tam ahaṃ brūmi brāhmaṇaṃ.

400. He who is free from anger, devout, virtuous, without craving, self-subdued, bearing his final body—him do I call a holy man. [18]

401. Vāri pokkharapatte va āragge-r-iva sāsapo,
yo na limpati kāmesu tam ahaṃ brūmi brāhmaṇaṃ.

401. Like water on a lotus leaf or a mustard seed on the point of a needle, he who does not cling to sensual pleasures—him do I call a holy man. [19]

402. Yo dukkhassa pajānāti idh'eva khayam attano,
pannabhāraṃ visaṃyuttaṃ tam ahaṃ brūmi
brāhmaṇaṃ.

402. He who in this very life realizes for himself the end of suffering, who has laid aside the burden and become emancipated—him do I call a holy man. [20]

403. Gambhīrapaññaṃ medhāviṃ maggāmaggassa kovidaṃ,
uttamatthaṃ anuppattaṃ tam ahaṃ brūmi
brāhmaṇaṃ.

403. He of profound knowledge, wise, skilled in discerning the right path and the wrong path, who has reached the highest goal—him do I call a holy man. [21]

404. Asaṃsaṭṭhaṃ gahaṭṭhehi anāgārehi c'ūbhayaṃ
anokasāriṃ appicchaṃ tam ahaṃ brūmi brāhmaṇaṃ.

404. He who holds aloof from householders and ascetics alike, and wanders about with no fixed abode and but few wants—him do I call a holy man. [22]

405. Nidhāya daṇḍaṃ bhūtesu tasesu thāvaresu ca
yo na hanti na ghāteti, tam ahaṃ brūmi brāhmaṇaṃ.

405. He who has renounced violence towards all living beings, weak or strong, who neither kills nor causes others to kill—him do I call a holy man. [23]

406. Aviruddhaṃ viruddhesu attadaṇḍesu nibbutaṃ
sādānesu anādānaṃ tam ahaṃ brūmi brāhmaṇaṃ.

406. He who is friendly amidst the hostile, peaceful amidst the violent, and unattached amidst the attached—him do I call a holy man. [24]

407. Yassa rāgo ca doso ca māno makkho ca pātito
sāsapo-r-iva āraggā tam ahaṃ brūmi brāhmaṇaṃ.

407. He from whom lust and hatred, pride and contempt have fallen off like a mustard seed from the point of a needle —him do I call a holy man. [25]

408. Akakkasaṃ viññāpaṇiṃ giraṃ saccaṃ udīraye
yāya nābhisaje kañci tam ahaṃ brūmi brāhmaṇaṃ.

408. He who utters gentle, instructive, and truthful words, who imprecates none—him do I call a holy man. [26]

409. Yo'dha dīghaṃ va rassaṃ vā aṇuṃ thūlaṃ subhāsubhaṃ
loke adinnaṃ nādiyati tam ahaṃ brūmi brāhmaṇaṃ.

409. He who in this world takes nothing that is not given to him, be it long or short, small or big, good or bad—him do I call a holy man. [27]

410. Āsā yassa na vijjanti asmiṃ loke paramhi ca
nirāsayaṃ visaṃyuttaṃ tam ahaṃ brūmi brāhmaṇaṃ.

410. He who wants nothing of either this world or the next, who is desire-free and emancipated—him do I call a holy man. [28]

411. Yass'ālayā na vijjanti aññāya akathaṅkathī,
amatogadhaṃ anuppattaṃ tam ahaṃ brūmi
brāhmaṇaṃ.

411. He who has no attachments, who through perfect knowledge is free from doubts and has plunged into the Deathless—him do I call a holy man. [29]

412. Yo'dha puññañ ca pāpañ ca ubho saṅgaṃ upaccagā
asokaṃ virajaṃ suddhaṃ tam ahaṃ brūmi brāhmaṇaṃ.

412. He who in this world has transcended the ties of both merit and demerit, who is sorrowless, stainless, and pure—him do I call a holy man. [30]

413. Candaṃ va vimalaṃ suddhaṃ vippasannaṃ anāvilaṃ
nandībhavaparikkhīṇaṃ tam ahaṃ brūmi brāhmaṇaṃ.

413. He who, like the moon, is spotless and pure, serene and clear, who has destroyed the delight in existence—him do I call a holy man. [31]

414. Yo imaṃ palipathaṃ duggaṃ saṃsāraṃ moham accagā,
tiṇṇo pāragato jhāyī anejo akathaṅkathī,
anupādāya nibbuto tam ahaṃ brūmi brāhmaṇaṃ.

414. He who, having gone beyond this miry, perilous, and delusive round of existence, has crossed over and reached the other shore, meditative, calm, and free from doubt, who by clinging to nothing has attained to Nibbāna—him do I call a holy man. [32]

415. Yo'dha kāme pahatvāna anāgāro paribbaje
kāmabhavaparikkhīṇaṃ tam ahaṃ brūmi brāhmaṇaṃ.

415. He who, having abandoned sense pleasures, wanders about as a homeless one, who has destroyed both sensual desire and continued existence—him do I call a holy man. [33]

416. Yo'dha taṇhaṃ pahatvāna anāgāro paribbaje,
taṇhābhavaparikkhīṇaṃ tam ahaṃ brūmi brāhmaṇaṃ.

416. He who, having abandoned craving, wanders about as a homeless one, who has destroyed both craving and continued existence—him do I call a holy man. [34]

417. Hitvā mānusakaṃ yogaṃ dibbaṃ yogaṃ upaccagā,
sabbayogavisaṃyuttaṃ tam ahaṃ brūmi brāhmaṇaṃ.

417. He who, having cast off the human bond and transcended the celestial bond, is delivered from all bondage—him do I call a holy man. [35]

418. Hitvā ratiñ ca aratiñ ca sītibhūtaṃ nirūpadhiṃ,
sabbalokābhibhuṃ vīraṃ, tam ahaṃ brūmi brāhmaṇaṃ.

418. He who, having cast off like and dislike, has become tranquil, rid of the substrata of existence, a hero who has conquered all the worlds—him do I call a holy man. [36]

419. Cutiṃ yo vedi sattānaṃ upapattiñ ca sabbaso,
asattaṃ sugataṃ buddhaṃ, tam ahaṃ brūmi brāhmaṇaṃ.

419. He who, in every way, knows the death and rebirth of beings, and is totally detached, blessed, and enlightened—him do I call a holy man. [37]

420. Yassa gatiṃ na jānanti devā gandhabbamānusā,
khīṇāsavaṃ arahantaṃ, tam ahaṃ brūmi brāhmaṇaṃ.

420. He whose track no gods, no angels, no humans trace, the arahat who has destroyed the cankers—him do I call a holy man. [38]

421. Yassa pure ca pacchā ca majjhe ca natthi kiñcanaṃ,
akiñcanaṃ anādānaṃ tam ahaṃ brūmi brāhmaṇaṃ.

421. He who clings to nothing of the past, present, and future, who has no attachment and holds on to nothing—him do I call a holy man. [39]

422. Usabhaṃ pavaraṃ vīraṃ mahesiṃ vijitāvinaṃ
anejaṃ nahātakaṃ buddhaṃ tam ahaṃ brūmi brāhmaṇaṃ.

422. He, the noble, the excellent, the hero, the great sage, the conqueror, the passionless, the pure, the enlightened—him do I call a holy man. [40]

423. Pubbenivāsaṃ yo vedī saggāpāyañ ca passati,
atho jātikkhayaṃ patto, abhiññā vosito muni,
sabbavositavosānaṃ, tam ahaṃ brūmi brāhmaṇaṃ.

423. He who knows his former births, who sees heaven and hell, who has reached the end of births and has attained to the perfection of supernormal insight, the sage who has reached the summit of spiritual excellence—him do I call a holy man. [41]

Index of Pāli First Lines

Index of English First Lines

A fool who knows his foolishness: 63
A monk is not an elder because his head is gray: 260
A striver-on-the-path shall overcome this earth: 45
A tamed elephant can be led into a crowd: 321
A victor am I over all, all have I known: 353
A worse taint than these is ignorance: 243
Abandoning the dark way: 87–88
All conditioned things are impermanent: 277
All conditioned things are unsatisfactory: 278
All things are not self: 279
All tremble at violence, all fear death: 129
All tremble at violence, life is dear to all: 130
Although he recites few sacred texts: 20
Although he recites many sacred texts: 19
An evil deed committed does not immediately bear fruit: 71
An evil deed is better left undone: 314
Any loose act, any corrupt observance: 312
Arise! Do not be heedless: 168
As a bee gathers honey from the flower: 49
As a fish when pulled out of water: 34
As a great flood carries away a sleeping village: 287
As a mighty flood sweeps away the sleeping village: 47
As an elephant in battle withstands arrows: 320
As from a great heap of flowers many garlands: 53
As upon a heap of rubbish: 58–59
Because he has discarded evil: 388
Before long, alas, this body will lie: 41
Behold this body, a painted image: 147
Beset by craving, people run about: 342–343
Better it is to live alone: 330
Better it is to live one day seeing the Deathless: 114
Better it is to live one day seeing the rise and fall: 113
Better it is to live one day seeing the Supreme Truth: 115
Better it is to live one day strenuous: 112
Better it is to live one day virtuous: 110
Better it is to live one day wise and meditative: 111
Better than a thousand meaningless verses: 101
Better than a thousand meaningless words: 100
Better than reciting a hundred meaningless verses: 102
Better than sole sovereignty over the earth: 178

ABOUT PARIYATTI

Pariyatti is dedicated to providing affordable access to authentic teachings of the Buddha about the Dhamma theory (*pariyatti*) and practice (*paṭipatti*) of Vipassana meditation. A 501 (c) (3) nonprofit charitable organization since 2002, Pariyatti is sustained by contributions from individuals who appreciate and want to share the incalculable value of the Dhamma teachings. We invite you to visit www.pariyatti.org to learn about our programs, services, and ways to support publishing and other undertakings.

Pariyatti Publishing Imprints

Vipassana Research Publications (focus on Vipassana as taught by S.N. Goenka in the tradition of Sayagyi U Ba Khin)

BPS Pariyatti Editions (selected titles from the Buddhist Publication Society, copublished by Pariyatti)

MPA Pariyatti Editions (selected titles from the Myanmar Pitaka Association, copublished by Pariyatti)

Pariyatti Digital Editions (audio and video titles, including discourses)

Pariyatti Press (classic titles returned to print and inspirational writing by contemporary authors)

Pariyatti enriches the world by

- disseminating the words of the Buddha,
- providing sustenance for the seeker's journey,
- illuminating the meditator's path.

Printed in Great Britain
by Amazon

38603697R00091